# HOUSE AND HOME
## MAKING THE BEST OF YOUR PROPERTY

# House *and* Home
# Making the best of your property

# CLIVE HOLLAND

Book Guild Publishing
Sussex, England

The information in this book is intended to be an introductory guide
and is not a definitive source of legal information.

First published in Great Britain in 2012 by
The Book Guild Ltd
Pavilion View
19 New Road
Brighton, BN1 1UF

Printed in Great Britain by
CPI Antony Rowe

A catalogue record for this book is available from
The British Library.

ISBN 978 1 84624 839 9

# *Dedication*

I would like to dedicate my first ever book to my late Mum and Dad, who, like all our Mums and Dads, are pretty special. (Never forget to tell them you love 'em.)

To my family for putting up with me being away so much every year filming and writing. I love you loads.

# Contents

## Chapter Six
## Can You Do it Yourself?

## Useful Resources

# *Thank you*

To you for buying my book.

The British public for their wonderful support from
the moment I began my career in television.

Carol Biss and all her fantastic team at Book Guild
Publishing for their help and support.

The BBC for having the faith and giving me wonderful opportunities.

The team at Mentorn Media for their continued support

Mick Henman MRICS, AB, MB Eng for the
building control and planning advice.

Ian Brandon for the mortgage advice.

Ian Oliver for the best fashion advice for big blokes
that I don't always listen to but should.

The top tradespeople of Great Britain, of which there are many, I
salute you and say that I will try to continue to starve the lifeblood of
the rogues by arming as many homeowners with advice on how to
avoid them, in the hope you will get the work you so richly deserve.

# Introduction

I have visited hundreds of properties and spoken to many disillusioned homeowners who have been the target of cowboy builders and I have witnessed the devastation that it causes. In many cases it hasn't just hurt the homeowners' pockets, it has mauled their emotions, too. I've seen the outcome drive wedges in relationships and cause rifts and heartache within the family structure. I try to give the best advice I can to the many millions of viewers who have watched me present property shows such as *Cowboy Trap* over the years, in the hope that it will prevent some of them from getting caught out. However, throughout my time touring the country in the last decade or so, or meeting homeowners at live events, the message I hear loud and clear, time and time again, is, 'We have watched your shows and seen you live and convinced ourselves that we would not make the same mistakes and take on board the hints and tips you give, yet we find ourselves in exactly the same position!' Many have asked if I could write a book that they can keep handy to use as a reference guide. People I meet and the thousands who contact me every year via email ask me the same question. So, here it is; I finally found some time between my filming commitments to write the book. It's not just about how to avoid the rogues, though. There is plenty of information for those considering buying a property for the first time and those who already own a property and want to move or improve. The book is packed with top tips and advice.

Sadly, as I write this book we are in pretty austere times; the recession is biting hard and the property market has hit a lull. As a result, many people are opting to renovate or extend their existing property rather than move on to something more suitable for their needs. If that's you, you've come to the right place - just as a home is a considered purchase, I'm really pleased you considered the purchase of my book. My aim is to help you every step of the way. Imagine you have a hold of my giant hand and I'll try to keep you safe. The final decision, however, must be yours.

First up, in Chapter One I have tackled some of the issues surrounding **buying a property**, particularly if you are looking at somewhere that may need renovation work. I've really homed in on the pitfalls to avoid, helping you make a purchase that will be an investment for the future rather than a money pit.

I always say that if you fail to prepare, you should prepare to fail, and in that spirit I have dedicated a whole chapter to **planning your renovation project**, which guides you through the red tape of planning permission, and includes advice on budgeting and ideas for how to find inspiration and devise a renovation that's right for you.

After over three years spent rescuing unwitting homeowners from the fallout left behind by unscrupulous trades people on my show, BBC1's *Cowboy Trap*, the perils of allowing un-vetted contractors into your home has become a subject close to my heart. In Chapter Three I draw on my experience in this area to give you a comprehensive guide to **hiring the right people for the job** in the first place, and to making sure your working agreement is clear cut. I've even drawn up a building works contract template guide for you – if I can't be there to watch over you in person, I'm going to make sure you have a contract in place from the get go! Of course, not all builders and trades people are out to get you – there are plenty of good guys out there who are ready to do a great job for honest pay. If you follow my tips, you will find them. The buck doesn't stop there, though. Once you've hired your renovation dream team you still need to pay attention to **making sure your project is a success** – from supervising the work to maintaining good working relations, and from getting that all-important completion certificate to what to do if something goes wrong. I have included some pretty awful stories from people who have asked for my help and advice over the years. I hope these will enable you to avoid falling into a similar trap.

Towards the end of the book I've included some detailed practical information about different types of home improvements – I call these **the nuts and bolts of home improvements**. So if you're planning on having a new kitchen installed, for example, you can flip straight to the relevant section and find handy tips galore. And all you wannabe DIY gurus are in luck because right at the end of the book there is a chapter where I ask, **'Can you do it yourself?'**. It's full of my very own insider top tips for small-scale home improvement projects.

I would like to thank you for buying the book and to wish you every success in living the property dream.

*Clive Holland*

# Chapter One

## Buying a Property

If you are in the market for a property, you might find your dream home, a place that ticks most of the boxes - location, price, character, features   but that needs a bit of work done. You might also specifically be looking for a property to buy at a knock-down price to do up and sell on. Or maybe you're a first-time buyer, and you're worried about having the wool pulled over your eyes, acquiring a property only to discover later down the line that there are existing problems which you will have to pay out to have fixed. Whatever your circumstances, you need to approach buying a house with your eyes wide open, wise to the pitfalls to avoid, and to make a realistic assessment of any work that needs to be done and the costs involved. This chapter will show you how to do just that.

## Let's Talk Finance

So what should you consider when buying a property? The first thing that should spring to mind is affordability: can you afford it? Basic and simple? Yes, I agree. Do the math in the first place and don't kid yourself, because if you do it will definitely end in tears. Don't let anyone force you into making a poor financial decision; you're a grown-up, so be honest with yourself and deal with it!

# Getting a mortgage

Unless you have recently won the lottery, had an inheritance windfall or you're a wealthy business tycoon (or maybe you married one, you lucky thing!), it's most likely you will need to take out a mortgage in order to buy your new or next home. There are whole books devoted to the ins and outs of financing a house purchase, and I don't have room to cover it all in this humble tome, but the basics go something like this:

- Consider the resources you have available, set a maximum figure you want to spend and stick to it.

- Go to a bank or building society and test the water – let their mortgage advisor crunch the numbers and give you an idea of what size of mortgage you can afford and all the available options open to you.

- All banks, building societies and bona fide mortgage lenders will require you to pass an affordability check.

- If your credit rating is good, you meet all the criteria and then decide to proceed, you will be required to pay around a minimum 10 per cent deposit.

- If you can afford to put down a larger deposit, say 15 per cent, your monthly repayment interest rate falls too, so you will pay less each month.

- Once you have paid the deposit you will normally pay back the remainder of the loan over a 25-year period. This period can of course be adjusted either up or down to suit you. The period of repayment can also be affected by the age of the person or persons requiring the loan.

Remember, interest rates will fluctuate throughout the life of your mortgage. Some lenders will offer a fixed rate for the first few years or you can have a tracker style mortgage which tracks the current base interest rate, or bank rate as it's known, set by the Bank of England.

Some tracker mortgages can be capped; this means there's a limit to the maximum amount of interest your mortgage rate can rise to, irrespective of how high the bank rate goes. If the bank rate goes down you will have the opportunity to pay more off your mortgage each month - that way you can take advantage of the low rate and minimise the total amount of debt payable if the rates go up. Most banks will allow you to switch your mortgage after the fixed period but many will charge. The same may apply to an early repayment of the outstanding balance, so check the small print.

You will need to do plenty of research and solicit expert advice before putting pen to paper. It's just a case of knowing which mortgage suits you best and the only way of doing that is talking to a mortgage advisor.

I would also suggest that you talk to your lender every couple of years to find out if you have the best deal available for you at that particular time. Your circumstances may change, either for better or worse. If it's for the better, you could talk to your lender about increasing your monthly payments to reduce your mortgage in the long term; you can always reduce the payments again in the future if your circumstances change for the worse. Whatever you do, do not ignore any financial problems you have during the fixed term - speak to your lender and get advice on how they can help you. For those of you reading this who already have a mortgage you have been paying off for a few years, ask yourself this question: am I getting the best deal possible? Don't just keep thinking about it, do something about it and ask questions. You may well be in for a surprise. If so, the drinks are on you! (Soft drinks, of course.)

For further information on the subject, go to the consumer section of the Council of Mortgage Lenders' website, **www.cml.org.uk**, or consult the mortgages and homes section of The Money Advice Service website, **www.moneyadviceservice.org.uk**.

The higher the deposit you pay the less risky the mortgage proposition is to the lender so the interest rates offered tend to be lower as a result.

# Example mortgage repayments calculation

According to national statistics, currently, the average price for a home in Great Britain is £169,000. So let's say the property you are going to purchase is £150,000.

If you put down a 10 per cent deposit (£15,000), that's £135,000 left to pay.

If you are a couple and you intend to purchase the property as 'tenants in common', the lender will take into consideration the individual gross earnings of each person. Usually one person earns more than the other – one of you might earn £30,000 per annum, while the other earns £15,000.

The lender will allow four times the higher earning gross and one time the lower earning gross:

4 x £30,000 = £120,000
£120,000 + £15,000 = £135,000

Over a 25-year term, the monthly repayments (with a 10 per cent deposit paid) would be £868.98. That's based on an interest rate of 5.99 per cent for a three-year fixed rate. However, if you managed to get the funds together for a 15 per cent deposit, you would pay £692.86 per month because you would have paid more of the overall total off and your interest rate would be lower at 4.28 per cent, again for a three-year fixed rate. (Figures from the Woolwich as of April 2012.) That is a pretty big saving.

Different lenders have different criteria; if both tenants in common are on similar incomes, then they may look to lend three times the joint income. My advice is to shop around and get the best deal. Don't get lazy and accept the first offer or get comfortable by using a lender you have banked with for years unless they are offering the best long-term deal.

# Budgeting for renovation work

If you are looking to buy a property that may need a certain amount of remedial or renovation work, or if you intend to extend the property, then you need to factor those things into your overall purchasing budget.

Budgeting is not an exact science, but there is one hard and fast piece of advice I can give you - if you can't afford the necessary renovation work, don't buy the property. Many people end up overspending because they want a property so badly that they overlook any repairs and work that needs to be done. Over the years I have spoken to many homeowners who have been totally unrealistic with their budget forecast. It truly is vital that you are realistic from day one. What exactly can you afford to have done? If you overstretch yourself you may well find you are in a downward spiral of a seemingly bottomless money pit!

You should make a list of the most important jobs to be undertaken and budget for each one accordingly. If it's a property that you are going to move into straight away, it's important that the structure is safe and sound before doing so. The property being wind- and watertight is a good start. Forget about the periphery stuff just yet, like what colour scheme to have or where the telly is going to go. If you are on a tight or limited budget you must do the important things first: property security, gas, electrics and plumbing in good working order, good double-glazing in place and loft insulation to the recommended depth to keep the heat in, the cold out and those all important bills down. Later, once you are happy, safe and soundly ensconced in your new home you can start to plan a step-by-step list of jobs to be done in order of importance and put it on the wall for all to see. For example, the kitchen, bathroom, etc. Set a do-able timescale and finance target, do not over stretch yourselves. Patience is a virtue, we are often told, and it will pay dividends in the long run, I promise. Consider the story of the hare and the tortoise and apply the latter's logic.

Of course, if you have shed loads of cash lying around and money is no object, then you're one of the few lucky ones who can just blitz a property from top to bottom without fear. However, in most situations that is just not the case. You can still achieve your dream; it just takes a little longer.

Time and time again I have seen people's dreams shattered, through no fault of their own, due to unforeseen circumstances such as one partner losing their job and having to sell up or, worst-case scenario, having their property repossessed by the mortgage/finance company. However, many have come a cropper through being unrealistic with their finances. I have witnessed couples and families being torn apart by the stress it brings as well as it having an effect on their health and general well-being. Nobody can budget for that – you just can't put a price on it.

It is always best to take someone who is experienced in the renovation business along with you to view the house. Try to avoid using a builder you are considering employing for the work at this stage as you may end up revealing how much money you have available (I'll explain why this is a bad idea later in the book). It needs to be someone who can provide objective, independent advice, such as a friend who works in the trade or someone who has had similar work done on their house and can give you an idea of the potential costs involved. A surveyor can give you a ballpark figure.

It is also useful to look at fully renovated like-for-like properties nearby and find out the current market value, to give you an idea of how much the house you're hoping to buy may increase once any renovation work is completed.

I will cover the subject of raising finance for home improvements a little later on, in Chapter Two, but I will give you some words of caution here: do not be tempted to add the costs of renovation work on to the mortgage unless it's absolutely necessary. Over the life of your mortgage period that additional amount could end up costing you three or four times as much. Again, your mortgage lender should give you impartial advice and guidance on a separate loan for the renovation works over a far shorter time period.

 *'It may seem like a minor point, but don't forget to budget for and factor in the costs of moving house, interior/exterior decorating, furnishings and garden etc.'*

# Choosing the Right Property

Once you have decided on a budget and know how you will finance your purchase, the search can begin. So, what sort of property are you going to buy? In my opinion, the house must work for you because you are working for it. It's no good just looking at a property and thinking, *well, it's not quite right but it will do*. The 'it'll do factor' is just not good enough - you've got to be sure. The decision you make now could be one you have to live with for a very long time.

## What are your needs?

You need to start your property search with a clear sense of priorities, so consider the following:

✐ **Do I want a bungalow, a flat, or a terraced, semi-detached or detached house?**

✐ **How many bedrooms and other rooms would I like, and what size?** *Consider the dimensions of the furniture you already own and measure up - although you can always buy new furniture to fit a new house, that can be a hassle and of course incurs extra costs, so it's worth thinking about whether you can accommodate what you have already.*

✐ **What about the location?** *Think about whether you would prefer it to be rural, semi-rural or on a housing estate, whether it is near to your place of work, close to public transport and road networks, what local amenities there are, research the local schools if you have children, and so on.*

✐ **Do I need room for parking?** *Think about how many cars will need to be parked at the property and whether you would prefer a garage, a drive or if you are happy parking on the road. In some instances you may require a resident's permit for on-road parking. Parking your vehicle on the road* *can increase the cost of insurance so check with your insurance company.*

✏ **Do I need a big garden, land or outbuildings?**

✏ **Check whether the property you are interested in is freehold or leasehold**
*Freehold means the house and land is yours once it has been paid for. With leasehold, you buy the rights to the house but the land is leased to you for a certain period of time - this can cause complications when it comes to planning permission for renovation work.*

✏ **Do I want the option to add an extension to the house if required?**
*Perhaps you would like the option to extend your house at a later date as your family grows. When viewing properties, take a look at nearby houses and see if they have extended. If they have, that sets a precedent and would make a planning permission application for similar work much more straightforward.*

Once you have collated all the information and everyone is happy, start by informing all the local estate agents of your needs. Send them a copy of your list of priorities so that they can be on the lookout for you too. Many hands make light work, after all.

*'I've always used this saying on my television show when it comes to sizing up. I call it the four Ms rule: measure, measure, measure, and just for good measure, measure again!'*

## What you should look out for

So, you've found a property you think you'd like to buy. It's so important that you have your head screwed on and although the price, aesthetics, property, location and so on are hugely important, you must look at the bigger picture. Don't be afraid to ask the estate agent questions and to take a really close look at the property, otherwise you'll just go headlong into making that purchase based on excitement alone. So before you rush in to the purchase of what may look like, on the surface, the house of your dreams, dig a little deeper and check out the following:

### ⇨ What are the neighbours like?

*Whatever changes you might have in mind for your house; the one thing you can't change is your neighbours. So to ensure you're not moving onto Student Party Central, ASBO Avenue or Crime Wave Close, make a few visits to the area at different times of the day. Park your car out of sight and wander past the house – you can get a general feel for the street and might even have the chance to speak to some of the neighbours. You will be amazed at the things they know – not just about the previous owners of the house you are looking to buy but about the history of the property itself and any problems there might have been with it. You may, however, get more than you bargained for, so like a good boy scout or girl guide, be prepared!*

### ⇨ Take a good look at the outside of the property

*Don't be in a rush to look inside, because if you ignore the warnings the inside could soon be on the outside anyway. Look out for cracks in walls as they may indicate subsidence – something you could definitely do without. Many lenders will not even give you a mortgage on a property that has subsidence, and the cost of underpinning and deepening or laying new foundations is enormous. Subsidence cracks are usually 1 mm or more in width, and often wider at the top than the bottom. If the crack has caused a windowsill or lintel to fracture, that is a bad sign, too. Not all cracks indicate subsidence, though – they could be the result of changes in temperature or humidity. Only a qualified surveyor can determine with certainty the cause of a crack. You should also check for trees sited too close to the property because their roots can cause mayhem to the foundations and drainage pipes.*

### ✏ Check the state of the roof.

*Look out for any missing or slipped tiles or slates. Does the flashing appear to be intact? If any tiles have been off for some time there could be water damage to the property that should easily be visible from inside. Does the roof look like it has a deflection (sagging)? If the house has a flat roof on any part of the building, try to get to a good vantage point where you can see whether the felt or roofing material looks tired and worn or has any breaches. Though you may be too far away to identify all problems, you will be able to form a general opinion on the state of the roof.*

### ✏ Are the sewers and drains in good shape?

*Problems with sewers and drains can lead to other serious issues, particularly subsidence. New builds have plastic pipes but many older properties have clay pipes which, over time, can crumble or split due to ground movement, and can also be damaged by tree roots growing through the pipe walls and causing blockages. Obvious signs that might indicate sewer and drainage problems are overflowing manhole covers and any unpleasant smells emitting from the property.*

### ✏ Keep an eye out for signs of damp.

*Rising damp is the most common form of damp to be found in houses, and it is caused by moisture from the ground travelling up through the walls. Damaged plaster and stained walls often betray its presence. Most houses have a damp proof course installed to protect against this, but in an older building it may no longer be effective, and a really old property may not have one at all, though it is possible to create a new one. A damp problem may also arise from water ingress through the roof or exterior walls, but the cause is not always easy to identify - a surveyor will recommend commissioning a damp report, to be undertaken by a specialist damp company. It is also possible to buy rot and damp detectors from the larger DIY stores should you fancy doing a bit of damp detection yourself.*

14

### ✏ Is there any indication of rot or woodworm?

*Fungal decay (dry rot and wet rot) is the result of damp and can cause serious problems if left untreated. Unfortunately it can be difficult to detect if present in woodwork that has been painted over. Tiny holes in woodwork may be evidence of an old woodworm attack that has already been treated, while fresh activity is usually indicated by the presence of a fine powder, which is produced by feeding larvae. Bear in mind that if there is a current problem it can be dealt with successfully in most cases, but you would not be able to live on the property while the work is carried out or for several weeks after completion.*

### ✏ Is the property energy efficient?

*Lack of insulation in walls, floor and loft space can lead to major heat loss and huge energy costs, so if the house is not properly insulated then the cost of adding insulation is something you will need to factor in to your overall budget. You may be able to look up in the loft to assess the insulation situation, but the question of wall and floor insulation will need to be left to the surveyor. Windows are also an area where heat can be lost, so you should look at their overall state and whether there is any double-glazing. If it is an older property that has been graded by English Heritage and, for argument's sake, it is grade 2 listed, you must bear in mind that there may be restrictions on the type of windows you are allowed to have installed.*

### ✏ Find out where the boundary lines are.

*The boundary lines are drawn up on the house deeds and clearly marked. It's important to know your boundary lines and who is responsible for any fencing or walling along that line, because when you buy a property you have to maintain the boundary and the sharing of costs - any changes you may want to make to your house in the future could be affected by this.*

15

## Be realistic

If the house is exhibiting some of the more worrying signs above, that may be enough to dissuade you from pursuing the purchase before you even get to the stage of paying for a property survey, in which case maybe I have already saved you some money! If you can see for yourself that there are significant problems that would cost you way over your budget to put right then there is no point even paying for a professional to confirm the fact – steer clear and resume your property search.

Buying a property that has a few things wrong with it at a good price and renovating it can be a great investment, and you could see the value of the property increase satisfyingly once the work is done. On the other hand, being too ambitious can lead to a money pit, and you could end up spending more money than if you had bought a properly renovated house. So my final advice to you is to be realistic about what you can achieve and what you can afford, and aware of the sorts of problems that shouldn't be undertaken lightly. You should also be honest with yourself about what things you will be happy to live with until they can be fixed – you will have to wait for planning permission and for builders to be available, and there may be other factors that may delay your project going ahead.

*Clive says...*

**'When it comes to buying a property, it's time to shackle the heart and put the head firmly in charge.'**

## Getting a property survey

If, after going through the checklist above, you still want to put in an offer, you must get a professional assessment of the property's overall condition. I cannot stress enough the importance of getting a property survey done before going through with the purchase. You might think, *Clive, come on, we've got a lot to be thinking about, and this is too much to ask!* It may cost you a pretty penny, but it could save you pounds in the long run, and compared to the overall amount you will be spending to buy the house in the first place, the cost of the survey really only represents a small percentage.

A survey is completely objective and independent, and its aim is to help you make an informed decision about the property based on the facts placed before you. It provides information on various things, including the state of the structure. Based on the findings of the survey, you can consider whether to cancel the sale, buy the property as it stands, negotiate a new price with the seller, or ask the seller to fix the problems before you buy.

Note that a property survey is different to the 'valuation' carried out by your mortgage lender, which assesses the value of the property and whether it's suitable for a mortgage and is not a detailed inspection of the property's condition.

The cost of a survey depends on which type of survey you get, and also on factors such as the type, size and value of the property you're buying or selling, as well as any extra investigations you may wish to have done on certain areas of the property. Below I have outlined the three main types of survey available and listed some of the problems they may uncover. The Royal Institution of Chartered Surveyors (RICS) has more information about the different surveys and how to choose the right one for you.

**RICS Condition Report**

This is the least expensive, but most basic, type of professional assessment available. It's best suited to conventional properties and newer homes that seem to be in a reasonable condition and are built from common building materials. It reports on the condition of the property only, flags up matters for your legal advisors and gives a summary of problems that need attention. It doesn't include advice or a valuation. It's also suitable for those wishing to sell their home.

**Homebuyer's Survey and Valuation (HSV)**

This survey is also known as a Homebuyer's Report and is performed to a dedicated framework set out by the Royal Institute of Chartered Surveyors (RICS). It is a nine-page form, which includes all the major sections of a property that are clearly visible to the surveyor. The aim of this type of survey is to provide a brief of what the overall condition of the property currently is and to identify which areas are in need of further tests or more detailed investigation, rather than reporting on every aspect of the building. Gas, drainage, sewers and electrical wiring are not included in the survey, so I believe in this case you should consider having further reports and analysis carried out in these areas. This survey is most suited to conventional type properties that are in a reasonable condition and are less than 2,000 square feet in size. It's cheaper than a building survey, but is not suitable for all properties, in particular very old, unconventional types, or where the buyer is planning renovation of the property. It is recommended that all buyers have a HSV carried out on the house they would like to purchase.

The HSV will include:

• A report on the overall condition of the property, assessing its major and minor faults and whether any of the major faults will need repairing, and the cost implications of such remedial works.
• An assessment of whether damp is present in the walls, the condition of the woodwork and whether woodworm is present.
• An assessment of the condition of damp-proofing, insulation and drainage. However, the drainage will not be tested.
• An estimated cost for rebuilding in the event the property should be destroyed. This is usually for building insurance purposes.
• Recommendations for any subsequent surveys and investigations that might need to be undertaken on specialised areas prior to any contracts being exchanged.
• An up-to-date valuation based on the surveyor's expertise and knowledge of the property market.

**Building Survey**
OK, time for the big one. It used to be called a structural survey but is now referred to as a building survey. This type of survey is far more detailed and provides an in-depth report about the condition of the property. It is

the most thorough one available and can take several hours to complete. The survey will examine all accessible parts of the property and can also target specific areas of concern that you would like the surveyor to report on. It is generally recommended for older properties, those that may be unusual in design, refurbished, redesigned and restructured, extended properties, as well as older self-build properties. Over recent years I've seen new-build homes that have deteriorated rapidly for one reason or another and that's why I strongly recommend the full survey every time.

The cost of the survey will differ according to the size of the property and its condition, the approximate value of the house, its location and which surveyor or company is employed to carry out the inspection.

Sometimes these surveys can be used instead of the basic mortgage valuation, but only if the surveyor you use is approved by the mortgage lender. The actual survey does not provide a valuation, but the surveyor will include one if you request it. However, it is more likely that the building survey will be done for other reasons, as it provides such an extensive survey compared to the HSV.

The building survey will include:

• Testing for the presence of damp in the walls, damp in the woodwork and whether woodworm is present, and the results of these tests
• Investigations into the condition of damp-proofing, insulation and drainage, although the drains will not actually be tested.
• Technical information on how the property was constructed, and all the materials used.
• Background information regarding the location of the property.
• All major and minor faults found within the property, the implications that these will have and how much the repairs for these defects will cost. For example: the presence of dry rot, any problems with the roof (loft space and timber structure, state of the flashing, whether there is water ingress, whether a new roof is needed), the U-value of the house (the extent of any heat loss from the building due to cavity insulation and windows and whether their timber needs replacing), the state of the footings, the condition of the brickwork and the state of the electrics.

## Fire break barriers

All terraced and adjoining properties should have party walls or fire breaks installed in their lofts to prevent fire and smoke spreading from one property to another through the void in the event of a fire. An unbroken void acts like a chimney, allowing fire and smoke to spread rapidly to the adjoining houses. This can make it very difficult for firefighters to contain the spread of the fire and bring it under control. Party walls also prevent would-be burglars moving easily from one property to another via the roof space and gaining access through loft hatches.

If you buy a property and the surveyor report reveals that the firebreak barrier does not exist, mortgage lenders and property insurers will usually insist that the firewall be installed before the new occupants take up residence. Anyone who has lived in this type of property for a number of years would be advised to check in his or her loft space. If you have an elderly friend or relative who has lived in such a dwelling for most of their life, it may be worth checking on their behalf. Because this is an installation that will benefit adjoining neighbours, it may well be worth having a chat with them to share the cost. You never know, it could turn out be a lifesaver. Remember to use a bona fide builder to carry out the work.

- Notification of any subsequent or special inspections for remedial work that may need to be undertaken.
- (In terraced houses) Whether there is a separating/dividing firewall in the loft to stop fire spreading from house to house.

## CASE STUDY

### *'To survey or not to survey?' There is no question!*

Having suggested just how important it is to hire a surveyor when purchasing a property, in particular an old property, here is an example of how one retired couple decided the risk of not getting one was worth taking.

Over the last decade or so I have visited hundreds of properties that have been wrecked by cowboy builders and rogue tradespeople. But of course I have discovered on my travels that some homeowners are pretty naïve too when it comes to hiring builders or making considered property purchases.

The couple in question I met a few years ago. They were retired and wanted to live out the rest of their years together in a fabulous refurbished development in a much sought-after area. They needed to sell their own property first and with the money from the sale and their retirement fund, then they would be able to pay for their dream two-floor maisonette outright. They visited the development on several occasions and chose the apartment they wanted, which was at the top of the Victorian building. The work was still a few weeks away from being completed. The sale of their old property was close to completion. Once the sale had gone through, they arranged to meet with the developers' selling agents to make an offer for the apartment. Sadly, the one they had set their hearts on had been sold and so had the next one down. In fact, they were both snapped up within days of going on the open market, such was the demand. The only one left available was the ground floor two-level maisonette. In their haste of not wanting to lose out on it, they agreed the full asking price there and then of over half a million pounds! Nothing was subject to a surveyor's report because the couple felt that it could possibly delay matters and they could lose out on the last apartment available. They also believed that because it was a full refurbishment of the old property with a very upmarket price tag everything would have been done to the highest of building standards. WRONG! Had they required a loan or mortgage agreement to make the purchase, the loan companies would have insisted on a report being carried out. They could have placed a deposit on the property to secure it whilst a survey report was carried out, but they did none of the above. Why? Because once again we had a heart-ruling-the-head scenario – the other apartments in the block had sold quickly, so they panicked! After contracts were exchanged and monies handed over, the happy couple eventually moved into their dream property. Little did they know the dream was soon to become a living nightmare!

For about a month or so they were really settling in and enjoying life together in their retirement palace. They experienced what they thought were little niggles with damp patches on the new plasterwork, and so on. The developers said that the fresh plaster needed a little longer to dry out. They were reassured by this information. That was until one fateful morning when the couple noticed a huge crack had appeared in one of the skirting boards in the bedroom. On closer inspection the timber was absolutely rotten and turned to dust in their hands when they touched it! They quickly realised that the rotting timbers around their dream maisonette had just been filled in and glossed over. Time and time again, they left messages for the developer who failed to return their calls. Alarm bells began to ring and their dream seemed to be falling apart. Better late than never, and on the advice of a close friend, they decided to call in an independent surveyor to do a full report on their property. The report didn't make very good reading at all. The surveyor discovered that their apartment was riddled with dry rot, wet rot and rising damp! It would require a further £30,000 to put everything right. It might have looked beautiful on the outside but it was rotten on the inside. For starters, all the floor joists would need replacing, and the plaster had to be hacked off all the way round the walls to just over a metre in height to allow for the damp injection to be carried out successfully. The list of remedial work appeared endless in their huge apartment.

The devastated couple were advised to take legal action against the developers to try and recoup the costs of the remedial work. Soon after they began legal proceedings, they were informed that the developer had liquidated the limited company that had carried out the refurbishments.

I do not wish to rub salt into their wounds or shout 'I told you so' from the rooftops. However, if they had stayed calm, not rushed headlong into buying their dream retirement home, managed the situation with their heads instead of their hearts and thought everything through properly, I have no doubt in my mind that this well educated and very savvy couple would have employed a surveyor to give it the 'peace of mind' once over.

No matter what your property type or age, employ a surveyor. It may save you some money in the short term not to have a survey carried out but it could save you shed loads of dosh in the long run if you do.

This case is a very extreme one. Sadly, it's not uncommon.

*'Remember: it's not what you can see, it's what you can't see that you need to worry about.'*

## Building surveyors

Building surveying has been around as a profession since the 1970s, undertaking projects from domestic extensions to major retail developments. Building surveyors offer advice on many aspects of design and construction, including maintenance, repair, refurbishment and restoration of proposed and existing buildings. They offer quality assessments and report on defects. They will offer ways of improving all kinds of buildings. As well as finding structural faults, building surveyors recommend solutions. They can advise on the feasibility of a building project, and how much it might cost to carry out, or how suitable a building could be for a particular purpose. Building surveying work can also involve drawing up detailed plans, and advising on whether a grant might be available for such works. Building surveyors instruct architects to prepare detailed plans and help provide estimates for the work. They are responsible for dealing with planning applications and advise on property law, building regulations and other legal matters such as health and safety. In building and contract disputes, building surveyors can act as an expert witness. Always remember to do your research to find the right one for you.

### Who can carry out a property survey?

A property survey should always be carried out by a qualified surveyor, for example, someone who is a member of the Royal Institution of Chartered Surveyors (RICS). They will have the letters MRICS, FRICS or AssocRICS after their name. All RICS surveyors are regulated and professional indemnity insurance is compulsory – which means that if you later find that a surveyor has missed a structural or other crucial fault with the house, you can complain to RICS and make a claim against them. You can find a qualified surveyor in a business directory or online by using the RICS website, **www.rics.org**. Make sure you shop around, do background checks on the surveyors and get three quotes for the work before signing someone up for the job.

# Buying a new-build

Before buying a newly built home, it's advisable to check whether the builder is registered with the National House-Building Council (NHBC), which is the leading warranty and insurance provider and standards setter for UK house building for new and newly converted homes. You can do this by calling NHBC's helpdesk on 0844 633 1000 or searching the register on the NHBC website, **www.nhbc.co.uk**. If your builder isn't registered with NHBC, check you'll be offered cover from another reputable company.

It's also a good idea to check the builder's reputation. Ask to look around properties they have built before and talk to previous customers. If possible, visit a working site – is it tidy and well managed? This will give you an indication of the builder's commitment to quality.

### Warranties for new properties

A building warranty is a guarantee that covers you if there are any defects that come to light after the sale. If you buy a property that is less than ten years old, it may be covered by a building warranty. Most new homes are protected by the National House-Building Council (NHBC) ten-year Buildmark warranty and insurance. However, some builders use other warranty providers – they should be able to give you full details of the property's warranty. The Local Authority Building Control (LABC) also provides warranties. You should ensure that the final building control certificate is available if the new property is not covered by an NHBC or similar warranty.

The warranty provider may offer to fix or pay out money if certain defects or problems arise with the property. Even if the house has a warranty, you should still get insurance, as the warranty will only apply to certain problems related to the construction of the building. You should make sure you know what types of defects are covered by the warranty and which are not. The warranty will usually transfer to the new owner if you sell the property within the period of the warranty.

## Energy Efficiency

If buying a property, you should be given an Energy Performance Certificate (EPC). This tells you about the property's energy efficiency rating and how you can make the property more energy efficient. You should be able to get an EPC from your estate agent.

### After exchanging on a newly built home

Once you have exchanged contracts, get the warranty documents from your solicitor and read them carefully before taking possession of your home. Make sure you inspect it carefully for any defects, snags, and so on. Wait until the home is fully completed before you move in, and once you have moved in, check your new home again thoroughly and report any defects in writing to the builder. Make sure you keep a copy if you are in dispute with the builder, and write to the appropriate NHBC office.

## Clive's Golden Rules

• Consider the resources you have available to purchase a property, set a maximum figure you want to spend and stick to it.
• Start your property search with a clear sense of priorities.

- If you can't afford any necessary improvements, don't buy the property.
- Don't be afraid to ask the estate agent questions, or to take a really close look at the property.
- Get a full building survey carried out by a certified surveyor.
- Get at least three quotes and check the surveyors' credentials before hiring someone for the job.
- Remember that based on the findings of the survey you can either cancel the sale, buy the property as it is, negotiate a new price, or ask the seller to fix the problems before you buy.
- If you intend to purchase a new build, make sure it's covered by a building warranty.
- If you buy a new build, make sure it's covered by a building warranty.

# Chapter Two

# Planning Your Renovation Project

Whether it is a loft or garage conversion, an extension, or simply adding a porch, any home improvement project involves big decisions. There are so many aspects to consider – from figuring out exactly what you want, to the red tape of planning permission and building regulations approval, to getting architect's plans drawn up and financing the project. That is why preparation is so important. From my experience of meeting hundreds of poor souls who ended up with a botched job, often the problems lie as much with their lack of planning as with any rogue tradesperson. So, before you even start your search for the right trades people, you need to make sure you have a solid plan in place.

*'Use the 5 P rule as your guide: 'Perfect Preparation Prevents Poor Performance!' Bear that in mind and you won't go far wrong.'*

## Putting Pen to Paper

The very first thing you need to do before commencing any project is to get a firm idea of what you want done, how you would like it done, how long it will take and how much it is likely to cost. It's time to put the kettle on, get out a notepad and pen (and a packet of biscuits!) and get it all down on paper.

# Get Inspired

So you've decided you would like a conservatory added to your house, but do you want it to be Victorian or modern style? Or maybe you are going to convert your garage into a living space – but do you want to use it as an office or an extra bedroom? And what about the tiles for that new bathroom, would porcelain, natural stone or mosaic work best? Most importantly, can you and your partner/mother-in-law/pet dog agree on all of the above?

Now, although I'm a big brute of a bloke and love getting involved with the somewhat mucky side of a property's construction and structural renovation, I also love the fluffy stuff and having hands-on involvement with the planning of interior designs. Just like property, interiors are very subjective and if there is more than one person involved in those plans who have very different opinions of what styles they like and dislike, I can pretty much guarantee a lyric from a well-known song will be playing in my mind: 'There may be trouble ahead...' In the past, interior designers would tear out their hair with frustration when, after spending weeks or months converting a client's wishes into reality, they would hear the words, 'Sorry, darling, I hate it!' Believe me, I've been there and it's not nice when you have to start all over again.

So before you take the plunge, here is a checklist of some of the things you should consider:

- **Who is going to be using the new/modified room, and what is it going to be used for?**
  *The purpose and user of the renovated area are an important consideration. For example, if you are having a loft conversion, will it be used as an extra bedroom or an office? If it's being used as an office, you might want to think about installing fitted shelving and storage for books and files, whereas if it's going to be a child's bedroom you might want to focus on safety features before the colour scheme and furnishings.*

- **Will it fit in with the rest of the property?**
  *You need to think about the style of your renovation in the context*

*of your house as a whole. In the case of a conservatory, for example, look at others in the style you are thinking of going for already in place at nearby houses to help you visualise how it will fit in with your own property. Trust me – a flashy modern-looking conservatory slapped on to the side of your Georgian period town house is going to stick out like a sore thumb. Remember that an extension or improvement should always add to the value of your property rather than take away from it. (I know you knew that!)*

### What size is reasonable?
*Be realistic about the size of your development and keep it in proportion with the size of the existing building. You don't want a conservatory to eat up too much of the garden, and an extension should be just that – 'extending' your living space rather than 'adding on'.*

### How can I create space?
*You don't necessarily have to go for an extension to create extra space in your home – there might be the option of knocking down a non-supporting wall to enlarge a room, for example, or removing a chimneybreast. And when planning an extension or converting a room, factor in ways of creating space and light to make the most of the new room – mirrors can give the impression of space and help to reflect light, while a carefully chosen colour scheme can also trick the eye into seeing a room as being bigger than it actually is.*

### Does it all have to be brand new?
*While the idea of popping to a well-known retailer and ordering a brand new, custom-made kitchen, for example, does hold its appeal, you can also pick up some great materials by being more creative with your sources. You can find some fantastic vintage items in second-hand sales, while reclaimed carcasses and suites can give you real value for money. It's all about shopping around and creating the feel you want for your house. There are some amazing reclamation yards around the country. A good way of finding them*

*is by searching on the internet. Some dealers are willing to sell off display units at a knock-down price when they change over to a new line in store, so it's worth keeping an eye out for these.*

✎ **Invest in a colour wheel.**
*This is simply a wonderful gadget and I really think that whoever invented it should be a millionaire by now or given an award, or both. As the name suggests, it is a wheel, around the edges of which are all the colours and shades of paint you can buy from the manufacturer. There is a dial in the centre that, when one end is pointed at the main accent colour you wish to use for a room, the other end will point to the perfect companion colour to complement that shade. Don't ask me how it works but it does, and sometimes you might not like the look of the suggested colour at first but trust me, it will work when you see it in practice. Lots of research has been carried out on this idea and I think it has paid off.*

✎ **Talk to other people who have had similar work done.**
*And to go and take a look at the finished product if possible. Ask them about their decision process and any problems they encountered along the way.*

## Create a mood board

One last important idea I would definitely add to the list above.

For the last ten years or so I have appeared at live shows like the Ideal Home Show and worked on the how-to theatre stages with many well-known faces from the world of makeover television as well as designers to the stars. A lovely designer I worked with one year introduced me and the audience to something called a 'mood board'. At first I thought it was just another gimmick. I soon realised that this tool would be invaluable in my line of work.

So, just exactly what is a mood board, I hear you cry. Well, a mood board is a great piece of kit for interior design and is an aid to planning for professionals and homeowners alike. Essentially, a mood board is a way of harnessing and visually illustrating inspiration and ideas in the shape of a simple flat board. Of course, you don't have to use one if you don't want to. But why not give it a go? For me, there is nothing more annoying than spending loads of time and effort on your designs and then suddenly realising all the textures, colourways and features in your newly decorated room don't actually work together after all. The great thing about the mood board is that it keeps you focused on what you like as an individual or group and what you do and don't really need in your design plan.

Here's how to get started then. Get hold of a big piece of sturdy card, hardboard or ply (your dad will have some in the shed, along with everything else he doesn't throw out just in case it comes in handy) around the size of an A1 sheet of paper. Some double-sided sticky tape or similar will come in handy too.

It's a great idea to have a theme to build your mood board around – it might be a design idea you have seen before and wish to recreate, or maybe some favourite furniture, a wallpaper design, soft furnishings or any colours and textures that you love. Whatever it may be, take a photo of it and glue it in the middle of your board where it will act as the main focus of the scheme.

Now begin to collect items to attach to your mood board – I'm talking pictures from magazines of furnishings you like, wallpaper samples, fabric swatches, paint charts, floor coverings, ceramic tiles, photographs – anything and everything that captures the 'flavour' of the room or rooms you're gathering ideas for. Interior design magazines and makeover shows on TV can really inspire you but don't be afraid to go with some of your own ideas too. Take a look at some of your favourite shops online and request a catalogue or two. Cut out any images that you like the look of and place them on the board. You can always replace them if you change your mind and want something different. Visit furniture stores and try to blag some swatches of your favourite sofa coverings or cut out a photo of the actual sofa from their brochures. Go to the tile shops and collect samples from their broken tiles that you like for walls and floors. Continue with wallpaper, carpets, laminate, curtains, and so on, until you have built up a collage specific to the room or rooms that you intend to transform. Some designers find it helps to put images of floor coverings near the bottom of the board and overhead lights near the top to create a semblance of how the room will come together.

There are no boundaries to your mood board and it can be as big and colourful as your imagination allows! Of course, the bonus is at this stage it has cost you zero in financial terms and you can change the design as often as you like until you arrive at the design that blows your mind. Once you've assembled the final palette, just take a step back and simply observe for a while. Place the mood board in the room and consider everything on it to make sure it really does float your boat in every way. Leave it out for friends and family to comment on and give you their thoughts. This could complicate things, however, because like I said in the beginning, it's all very subjective. Remember, the people who live within the space that's being made over must make the final decision. Simply remove anything that you are not 100 per cent sure about.

When you're happy with your mood board, take a photo of it, which will be handy to carry around with you when you begin to shop and place your orders.

Good luck – I'm sure you will enjoy the experience and the fruits of your labour.

## Show Me the Money!

Now that you have an image of your dream loft conversion, living room or new bathroom, it's time for a reality check – can you afford it?

You need to estimate just how much the work is going to cost and figure out whether you have the finances required. Don't make the mistake of overstretching yourself, because in my opinion, that's the first warning bell.

You might find you need to compromise and scale down on certain items to reduce the overall cost, but your priorities should always be health and safety, functionality and durability. Don't be tempted to cut corners on window installation in your loft conversion so that you can afford to put down a lush deep pile carpet, for example, because it could cost you more in the long run when you get a massive gas bill because you are losing heat through the window, or if it's of such poor quality that it lets the rain in.

Here are some of the things you will need to factor into your budget:

- **Professional fees for your architect/designer/surveyor/ structural engineer as required**
  *These will vary depending on the work involved and on you chasing the best value quote.*

- **Planning permission application costs**
  *Go to **www.planningportal.gov.uk** and use the handy online fee calculator. When it comes to building regulations charges, these will vary from council to council. Remember to seek advice regarding such charges with your local council.*

- **Margin of error**
  *You need to make allowances for extra unexpected costs, as much as 10 per cent of the overall cost of the project. This will come in handy if, say, a structural problem is uncovered during the build, or if you have to pay your architect to revise your plans during the application process.*

- **Cost of materials**
  *You can either allow the builder/relevant tradespeople to source materials and include the costs on the quote breakdown, or you could go directly to the merchants yourself, thus ensuring you have control over the cost of materials. Builders' and plumbers' merchants and electrical wholesalers may agree to open an account subject to a credit check, usually a 30-day account, which might include a discount for early settlement if you pay your bill before the 30 days are up; every little helps, you know!*

- **Labour costs**
  *The amount you will have to pay your builders and any other*

*tradespeople involved in work on the project, such as plumbers, electricians, painters, and so on.*

🖉 **Skip hire and waste removal**
*Shop around for skips, and don't underestimate how much waste there will be. Hire the big one! Ask the company exactly what you can dispose of as they can fine you if you put banned materials into the skip - paint tins, for example, now have to go to metal recycling plant. You should also check with the local council whether permission is required to site the skip on the road, if that is necessary, and there may also be a charge for this.*

As well as figuring out how much it's all going to cost, you need to think about how you are going to finance the project. If you don't have the amount required already saved in the bank, here are some options.

For an amount of up to £5,000, you could use 0 per cent interest rate credit cards - but make sure you pay it all back before the fixed 0 per cent period ends. Some credit card companies may offer you a higher maximum figure but please be careful. You could extend the loan even further if you transfer any balance over to another 0 per cent credit card before the deadline expires on the old one. You may incur small one-off charges for the use of these cards but that's nothing compared to the sort of interest a loan would burden you with.

For larger amounts, from £5,000 upwards, you could look into taking out a separate short-term loan on a fixed rate, but if you do, be sure to shop around for the best interest rate.

Another way to raise finance is to release further funds against the property. Typically lenders will lend up to 80 per cent of the property value, normally as a separate entity to the main mortgage, which means it can be done over a different/shorter term to the main mortgage. Raising finance in this way is cheaper than taking out a personal loan from an interest point of view but the borrowing would be secured against the property.

If there is insufficient equity in the property to allow the release of funds then you could borrow the necessary amount from other sources in the hope that the renovation work will increase the value of the property, allowing you to release funds at a later stage to repay any loans taken out, as long as it falls within 80 per cent or the new value.

My top tip is; save hard and make sacrifices for what you want. If you run two cars, find out if you can make do with one for a while. Reduce going out so often and find other ways to entertain yourself indoors. Monitor your food bills, cut back on your heating costs by simply reducing an hour or so on the central heating timer. Cut down on the number of electrical items left on standby overnight and pay attention to lights being left on and phone chargers being left plugged in. Over a period of one year, you will be amazed at how much you can save. In fact, have a period of being so tight that you only breathe in!

## CASE STUDY

### *Budgeting bodge*

Here is one of the cases I was called to see a few years ago that staggered me. This particular lady decided that she wanted a ground-floor extension to the rear of her property to create a smart new kitchen-diner she had long dreamed about. She took on an extra part-time job in the evenings and saved hard for her dream. So far, so good. During this period she invited four different builders to give her a general idea of what it was likely to cost. By her own admission, she was a million miles away from being able to afford it one year on from her grand idea. Then one day while at work she was talking to a colleague about how she felt she would never be able to afford her dream, when her colleague said, 'My mate's brother is a builder, shall I get him to pop round?' She thought there would be no harm in getting a quote. So began a chain of catastrophic events that would end in financial ruin for this poor woman.

Error one, she let him in her house. Warning bell one, he came on a bike because he had lost his licence through drink driving. Warning bell two, he stank of booze. Warning bell three, he claimed he could do everything from the foundations to the brickwork, roof, plastering, plumbing, woodwork, electrics, gas, tiling, painting and kitchen fitting.

(Time for a reality check, me thinks?) According to the homeowner, this chap was in his mid-twenties so if he really was qualified to do all these various disciplines he would be closer to retirement than school age! By the way, error two had already taken place by this time; her heart was leading the way and not her head. Warning bell number four was coupled with error three when this so-called builder said, 'You won't need any permission from the council to build this, it's too small.' (You can add the error and warning bells bits in yourself from here on in, I'm losing track; in fact, you can add the *Titanic's* foghorn in too, just for good measure!)

The price he quoted for the completed extension was exactly the amount she told him she had saved up... Funny, that. The figure was less than half of the lowest price quoted by the other builders, who had all said the extension would need planning permission and building regs consideration. At the time, the homeowner was delighted. However, delight would soon turn to despair. The build ran over time due to the so-called builder having every excuse under the sun for not turning up for more than two days at a time. 'I've got a cold/bad back/sprained wrist' or 'I can't come on site today because I've got a bone in my leg.' (I made the last one up!) He built the extension without seeking planning permission or building regulations approval over a sewer inspection pit, the foundations were less than 65 mm deep in places, he used no wall ties to tie the inner leaf to the outer leaf of brickwork, he didn't put insulation in the cavity, roof or floor, nor did he install a damp course. The list goes on and on.

He demanded more money to come back and finish the job, too. The homeowner duly obliged by taking out a loan from an online loan company with a massive rate of interest on the repayments. Even though she could see the work was shoddy at best, she was now not thinking straight at all and was too embarrassed to ask for help. The local planning and building regulations officers eventually came to look at the work on a tip-off from one of the neighbours who were concerned that one of the walls was leaning towards their garden. The so-called builder never returned. The local council condemned the extension and it had to be pulled down.

That lady cried a billion tears. Please let this be a lesson to all – you must have a realistic budget and ensure that any builder you hire to undertake the work sticks to that budget. A contract must be in place before work commences and you must find out if your build requires planning permission. Never throw money at a problem, hoping that will make it go away and all will be well in the end – you will just be throwing good money after bad. It's not like a sweet fairy tale ending where they all live happily ever after. Chances are your story will end with, 'And they all limped heavily ever after!'

# Timing is Everything

Once you know what you want and how you are going to pay for it, it's important to draw up a rough timetable of when you expect things to happen. You need to think about when would be the ideal time for work to take place – for example, if part of your house is going to be exposed to the elements during a loft conversion or extension, then it's better to time the work to coincide with the warmer months. Of course there's no controlling the weather and some years it's been known to rain all summer, but it makes sense at least to avoid major renovation work during the freezing winter months. If you are having a new bathroom or kitchen fitted, you might not want that to coincide with busy family visiting periods, such as Christmas. And it sounds obvious, but consult your diary first – you don't want to be away on a two-week sun-fest in Spain leaving the builders to their own devices while they get stuck in to your garage conversion.

I'll go into planning permission in more detail in the next section, but as a rough guide it takes eight weeks to come through, and once approved your plans are valid for three years, so that means you don't have to rush into starting the work immediately.

Here are some of the stages that you will need to factor in to your timetable:

- **Getting an architect to draw up plans**
  *Roughly eight weeks.*

- **Applying for planning permission**
  *Eight weeks if it doesn't have to be revised, allow an additional eight weeks if the plans have to be amended and resubmitted.*

✏ **Builder/tradesperson availability**
*The right tradesperson is worth waiting for, and if they are good at what they do they will be in demand so you might have to bide your time a little.*

✏ **Building/renovation work**
*The predicted timescale within which the work will be undertaken should be factored into your quote and contract (see Chapter Three), but you should also allow some time for unforeseen problems and delays.*

✏ **Finishing touches before a renovated room is fit for use**
*once any building work is completed there is still the cosmetic interior work to allow for, such as painting and decorating, and fitting carpets. Remember that flooring should be virtually the last thing to go in, to avoid damage during painting and drilling for fittings, etc.*

## Drawing up Plans

Once you have a good idea of what changes you would like to make to your home, you need to find yourself an architect to draw up the technical specifications which will be submitted with your planning permission or building regulations applications as 'supporting documents'. Architect drawings are not required in all situations – for example, when taking a non-supporting wall down. In all cases you should still check with your builder first whether they believe plans are necessary, but don't just take their word for it – contact your local planning office and they will be able to give you a definitive answer.

There are various supporting documents required for planning permission applications, depending on the type of consent you submit (see **The Red Tape** below), but a site location plan and a block plan are required for all application types.

## Site location plan

This is sometimes referred to as a 'location plan', and it shows the proposed development in relation to the surrounding properties. It has to be based on an up-to-date map and at an identified standard metric scale (typically 1:1,250 or 1:2,500). The proposed development site should be outlined in red, while any other land belonging to the applicant that is close to or adjoining the site needs to be outlined in blue.

## Block plan

Rather confusingly, this is sometimes called a 'site plan', and it shows the proposed development in relation to the property boundary.

Block plans are usually drawn up to a scale of either 1:200 or 1:500 and should include:

• The size and position of the existing building (and any proposed extensions) in relation to the property boundary
• The position and use of any other buildings within the property boundary
• The position and width of any adjacent streets

## Hiring an architect

You can find a qualified architect by visiting the Architects Registration Board website at *www.arb.org.uk*. You will find lots of information on there regarding the reasons why you need to employ a qualified architect, and there is also a searchable public register of over 33,000 qualified and certified architects. I would also highly recommend consulting the Royal Institute of British Architects (RIBA) website, *www.architecture.com*. It's also worth checking with The Institute of Architectural Technicians too. In recent years there has been a rise in people seeking architect qualifications abroad in countries where they can come by them much more quickly and cheaply. International standards of training differ, so by choosing a RIBA certified architect you can be assured that they meet the relevant legal professional requirements.

As you will read in more detail in Chapter Three, I always recommend getting at least three quotes, comparing prices and doing background checks before hiring anyone. The same applies should you need to hire an architect or a designer, or a structural engineer to help plan any large-scale structural work. In the case of an architect, you can check their reputation by asking to take a look at any completed work for which they provided the plans.

Bear in mind that if your planning application is returned to you stating that revisions need to be made to the plans before resubmitting, you will then have to pay the architect to make those adjustments. My tip is, when the architect has drawn up the plans in the first instance, ask them if they think there are any areas that could potentially cause problems with gaining planning approval. An architect will have a good idea of what sort of things may be an issue. If they say no, get that in writing from them – then if it turns out that permission issues do arise, the architect should not charge for making the necessary amendments to the plans.

# The Red Tape

Your plans are drawn up, the money is waiting in the bank and the vision of your new improved home is firmly planted in your mind... I bet you're raring to get started? If only it were that simple. First, you have to deal with the boring bit – the paper work. Luckily I'm here to help you navigate your way through local authority officialdom. It's not as scary as it sounds, promise.

## What are planning control and building regulations?

So what is the difference between planning control and building regulations? (I knew you were going to ask.) At first glance, it may appear that building regulations and planning control are nothing more than extra stumbling blocks that you have to negotiate in a minefield of restrictions that seem to be getting in the way of your build. However, without guidance and regulation, our landscape would be littered with ugly properties just placed anywhere and unsafe constructions. Planning control and building regulations are actually two separate sections of building law:

**Planning control** deals with the current permissible use of land, the appearance of the proposed building and the effect or impact the proposal will have on the environment and surrounding properties.

**Building regulations** are legal requirements that apply in England and Wales to promote adequate standards for most aspects of domestic, commercial and industrial building construction, including structural stability, fire resistance, moisture resistance, the health and safety of people in and around buildings, energy efficiency, the needs of all people, including those with disabilities, to allow access, ingress and the ability to move around buildings easily. These regulations are laid down by parliament and contained within separate documentation for practical and technical guidance on compliance. The documents are referred to as 'Approved Documents'.

Certain types of development will require planning permission but may not need building regulation, and vice versa.

## Do I need planning permission?

Sadly, some people don't realise that making alterations to their property or making a change to its use will require permission. Others do, but they want to avoid the hassle of making an application and so don't follow the proper process.

If you fail to obtain the necessary planning permission for a development, the local authority can force you, as the owner of the property, to take whatever actions necessary to remedy the breach of planning law. In the best-case scenario, this would mean making a retrospective application for permission and, if you are fortunate, it being granted. In the worst case, they could insist on the works illegally carried out being removed. The planning authority may, in some instances, prevent you from using the property for an unlawful purpose.

In the first instance, the local authority will contact the owner of the property to advise them to remedy the breach but, if they fail to do so, they will serve something called an 'enforcement notice'. This gives the owner six months to comply, and failure to do so will result in the local authority carrying out the removal of the offending and illegal work themselves at the owners' expense as well as issuing a fine of £25,000. Failure to pay the fine or the cost of the work can result in imprisonment!

Even if your unpermitted development were to pass by unnoticed, it would definitely come to light in a property survey should you wish to sell and would need to be addressed at that stage. In my opinion, it's just not worth taking the risk.

Works classed as 'development' under the Town and Country Planning Act 1990, and which require planning permission include:

- The carrying out of building, engineering, mining or other works in, on, over or under land
- The making of any material change in the use of any buildings or land
- Any demolition works
- A rebuild
- Alteration to structures
- Additions to existing buildings

*'Building regulations and rules on planning permission can be amended from time to time and it's important that you keep yourself up to date.'*

## Permitted developments

There are some instances where planning permission is not required, and these are known as 'permitted developments'. If you think that your planned improvement might come under this category, your first port of call should still be your local planning authority and building regulation department for professional guidance on local policy. It is always best to double check, and if possible get something in writing from the local authority stating that your planned development is permitted and does not require planning permission.

The following are permitted developments, provided you stay within the guidelines and follow the relevant building regulations:

- Loft conversion (subject to size)
- Basement conversion to living space
- Some conservatories, porches, property extensions, garage conversions

However, just because a development is permitted without planning permission, it doesn't give you carte blanche to do whatever you like! Certain guidelines and regulations must be observed, and once again, you should check with your local planning authority and building regulations department.

## Loft conversion

In the case of a loft conversion, for example, there are guidelines that state that:

- Any additional roof space created must not exceed 40 m² for a terraced property and no more than 50 m² for a semi-detached or detached house.
- No part of the extension can be higher than the existing roof ridge.
- Balconies or platforms are not permitted.
- Loft conversions are not permitted on designated land (heritage sites, conservation areas, places of outstanding beauty and national parks).
- You must install a fire escape and observe relevant fire safety measures.

There are various other guidelines on loft conversions, and one of them is rather more surprising. Bats are a protected species and often take up residence in loft spaces and they don't pay board! If you think you may have bats in your belfry, you will need to call in a surveyor and you may have to apply for a special licence. Crazy, I know, but those are the facts.

## Basement conversion

Converting a basement into a living space can also fall under the heading of permitted development, provided, amongst other things, the following:

- It is not a separate dwelling unit.
- The usage is not being significantly changed.

- You don't intend to install a light well which would alter the external appearance of your home.
- The foundation may also need to be underpinned (which will require building regulations approval).
- Party walls need to be considered if the property is terraced or semi-detached.

Various other building regulations will apply, concerning, for example, fire escape routes, damp-proofing, electrical work, water supply, ventilation, the height of the ceilings, and so on.

# How to apply for planning permission and building regulations approval

So, how does planning permission work and how do you make an application?

First of all, you are going to need good dialogue with your local planning and building regulations departments. Book an appointment before you submit an application to make sure you understand the local planning authority's requirements and to say hello, of course.

You can register to apply online at **www.planningportal.gov.uk**, or you can download the relevant form from the website, then fill in and post your application to your local authority. Every local authority in England and Wales accepts online planning applications from the Planning Portal, and the advantage of completing a form online is that you are prompted to answer only questions pertinent to your application. Once completed, the form is sent directly to the local planning authority for processing. There are various types of application, so you will need to figure out which one applies to your proposed work before you get started.

### Householder planning consent

Householder planning consent is the one that covers proposals to alter or enlarge a single property, including works within the boundary of a house and the land belonging to it. It covers such projects as: extensions, conservatories, loft/garage conversions, dormer windows, porches, carports and outbuildings. Planning permission is not always required for this type of work, in which case it would fall under the permitted development rules that I mentioned earlier.

## Full planning consent

Full planning consent forms are for a detailed and in-depth application, which excludes householder development. It does include building, engineering or other works in, on, over or under the land or creating any material change in the use of any building or other land. This application should be used for: works relating to a flat, or to change the number of dwellings (for example, flat conversions or a separate house in the garden); changes of use to part or all of the property to non-residential, including business use; any construction outside the garden boundary, such as stables in a separate paddock.

## Outline planning consent

Outline planning permission seeks to establish whether the scale and nature of a proposed development would be acceptable to the local planning authority before a fully detailed proposal is put forward. This type of application allows for less detail about the proposal to be submitted. The moment outline permission has been granted, you will require approval of the details before you can begin the works. These details will be the subject of a 'reserved matters application' at a later stage.

## Other types of consent

Other types of consent include:

• Conservation area consent - required for certain developments within conservation areas.
• Listed building consent - required if demolishing or altering a listed building in such a way that affects its character as a building of special architectural or historic interest.
• Consent under Tree Preservation Orders - concerns works proposed to trees subject to a tree preservation order (TPO).

## Lawful Development Certificate

You can apply for a lawful development certificate (LDC) to prove that an existing or proposed use of a building is lawful or that the proposal doesn't require planning permission. I think it's a good idea to obtain one, if only for peace of mind – but also just in case some busybody wants to poke their nose in and cause a bit of trouble! Property envy can cause some people to play dirty, shall we say.

## The Building Notice Route

Oh yes, more choices – and we haven't even started building yet!

Rather than submitting a full plans application as detailed above, there is the cheaper option of submitting a building notice to your local authority building control service instead, which does not require costly detailed architect plans to be drawn up and no approval notice is issued. It is designed to enable some types of building work to get under way quickly. Remember, building regulations approval will be required.

I feel this system is best suited to smaller projects, although there is a good chance that you may still be asked to provide plans if the job is not a straightforward one, and it can only be applied to domestic work.

However, there are some instances where building notices cannot be used. These are:

• For building work which is subject to section 1 of the Fire Precautions Act 1971 or Part II of the Fire Precautions (Workplace) Regulations 1997
• For work which will be built close to or over the top of rain water and foul drains shown on the 'map of sewers'
• Where a new building will front onto a private street

If you do decide to go down the building notice route, you must be confident that the work will comply with building regulations, otherwise

46

you risk having to correct any work at your local authority's request. This means you do not have the protection provided by the approval of a full plans application.

Once you have submitted a building notice and informed your local authority that you are about to start work, the work will be inspected as it progresses, and you will be advised by the authority if the work does not comply with building regulations. If before the start of work, or while work is progressing, your local authority requires further information (such as structural design calculations or plans) you must supply them as requested.

A building notice is valid for three years from the date it is submitted to the local authority, after which it will automatically lapse if work has not commenced.

Do take note: a local authority is not required to issue a completion certificate under the building notice procedure, and because no full plans are produced it is not possible to ask for a determination if your local authority says your work does not comply with building regulations.

*'Please DO NOT attempt to go down this route unless you know exactly what you are doing. Keep your local authority for planning and building regulations on your side. A good working relationship between you will pay dividends! Get the names and contact details of your local authority planning and building regulations officials and store them in your phone. The 'full plans application and building regulation approval' route allows both you and your builder to know exactly what is expected.'*

## The decision process

Once you have submitted your planning application or building notice, you can begin the work after you have given the relevant departments two days' notice. However, I do feel it's best to wait until you have had the go-ahead from the planning office and building regulations department, especially if you are undertaking major work that has required a full plans application, otherwise you will be working at your own risk. If you fail to get permission, the local council can have the work removed.

The decision-making process works something like this:

- The local planning authority will give the application the once over to check that it has been completed properly.
- The application will be registered for consideration.
- The planning authority will publicise the application and consult on it where necessary.
- The application will be considered and decided on within an eight-week time frame. However, if it's a complex or large project, it could take longer. If you ask nicely at the planning office (take them some sticky buns) they should be able to give you a rough idea of the time frame.
- Should the authority fail to come to a conclusion within the standard eight weeks, they will ask for your written consent to extend the time period. If they fail to do so, you can appeal to the first secretary of state but be warned, it can take months for such appeals to be resolved and I think the best policy is to reach an amicable agreement with the local planning authority. (Remember, make it a Friday and take buns!)
- You will normally be notified of any decision by post. If your application is given the go-ahead with conditions attached, you will have to get your architect to make any necessary amendments to your plans before resubmitting. If your application is turned down and you would like to contest the decision, you will have to speak with the 'mighty cheese' and try to get the matter resolved by a planning inspector. (That's more sticky buns!) On the odd occasion it has been known that the first secretary of state will make the final decision. (A tray of sticky buns!)
- If you are successful and your application is granted, it will have an expiry date in accordance with the planning laws. Unless your permission states otherwise, you will have three years from the date of permission to get cracking with the work and if you haven't started by the time the third year elapses, you will have to reapply. The good news, however, is you can apply for a further two-year extension as long as you do so before your old permission expiry date runs out.

## Notification of development

Be aware that once the planning authority has received your planning application, they have to post notice. This means your application will appear on the local authority planning website, in the public notices section of your local newspaper, on street furniture, as a yellow site notice displayed on the site boundary, and directly to neighbours whose homes could possibly be directly affected by your plans. This allows 21 days for any objections to those plans to be heard and discussed by the planning committee.

**Clive says...**

*'If you notice any building work going on in your neighbourhood for which planning notices have not been posted within 100 feet of the property, call your local planning authority and let them know.'*

## Plan ahead or stay in bed!

If I haven't already convinced you of the importance of gaining relevant planning permission, then this very sad story should seal the deal. A lovely but very distressed couple with children contacted me to ask for advice as they felt they had nowhere to turn. They had decided to add an extension to their house to accommodate their growing family. They knew little about planning applications, and when a builder came along and gave them a cheap quote they were delighted.

This builder was a cowboy of the very worst kind. He waited for them to leave the house and started work without their permission, and without planning permission either! The poor couple came home from work to find their house transformed into a building site. The work he had done in preparation for the extension had undermined the roof on the existing house, and so they were scared to stop him working and allowed him to carry on. It later transpired that he had done this to numerous other people in the area.

The builder reassured them that he was getting planning approval and that the building control officer was coming the next day, and sure enough he did, all kitted out in a high-vis jacket, hardhat and what looked like the right documentation. However, the impostor had pulled the wool over the couple's eyes once again – the 'building control officer' later turned out be his brother.

Building work progressed and the couple were left with a two-storey extension with inadequate footings, no windows, a leaking roof, cracks in the walls, dodgy electrics and gas, and it cost them over £50,000! When I saw the place for the first time I was so shocked by the state of the build that I quickly declared it a complete no-go zone – I even made sure I told the postman not to step foot near the house! I contacted the local council and it turned out they knew nothing of the build.

Luckily for the couple I was able to contact a structural engineer and surveyor to draw up a detailed report on the extension to try to save them from the cost of ripping it up and starting again. An underpinning company came in to save the day and prevented the structure from being taken down completely. Emergency work on the gas and electrics was carried out too by 'gas safe' and qualified gas and electrical engineers respectively. It was wonderful to put this family's minds at ease but they were totally broke, both financially and emotionally.

It just goes to show that planning control and building regulations aren't just there to make your life difficult – they are there to protect you from ending up with a home that is unliveable and unsafe for you and your neighbours.

## Clive's Golden Rules

- Think carefully about what you want from your renovation project and create a mood board to help visualise your ideas.
- Don't overstretch yourself financially.
- Have the necessary finance in place before beginning the project.
- Draw up a rough timetable of when you expect things to happen.

- Get a certified architect to draw up plans.
- Make sure you apply for necessary planning permission.
- Have a good working relationship with your local planning authority
  – sticky buns always help!
- Have a contract in place before work commences.

# Chapter Three

---

# Hiring the Right People for the Job

If there is one message you take on board from this book, and that has come through loud and clear through my years of meeting home-owners hit hard by rogues, it's the importance of sourcing reliable, skilled, reputable tradespeople to undertake any work in your home. You wouldn't leave your children with an un-vetted nanny, would you? Neither would you let a dodgy backstreet dentist pull one of your teeth, I'm guessing? So why would you allow someone you're not 100 per cent sure of loose on your precious home? It just doesn't make sense. And yet every year thousands of people in the UK lose thousands of pounds and are caused untold heartache and stress by rogue tradespeople. Take my advice – don't be one of them! It's not just about hiring the right people for the job, though – it's also about making sure both parties have a clear understanding of the project, to avoid misunderstandings further down the line. To find out how to hire your building dream team, step this way, please...

## The Search is On

So you've planned your project, saved enough money and submitted your planning and building regulations application, which hopefully will be approved by the time eight weeks are up. This is not a time to rest, however; it's a time to start researching the trades.

# Who do I need for the job?

Before you even begin your search, you need to assess which trades-people will be required for the project. Don't be tempted to go along with builders who tell you they can bring in all the trades. It might seem like a good idea, saving you the trouble of all that extra tedious research and quote comparing. But if you want total success for your project, you have got to decline their offer.

Time and time again homeowners have told me about how they paid a main contractor, who had said they would sub-contract the other trades out, only to discover later that the main contractor never passed the payment on to the other trades. In most cases, once the main contractor's work was done and they had been paid they would disappear without trace and the other traders, rightly angry at being out of pocket, would come knocking on the homeowner's door to tell them that if they didn't pay up again, directly to them, they wouldn't complete the work.

As the old saying goes, 'Jack of all trades, master of none.' You want the very best for your project, and anyone who claims to be able to undertake a variety of specialist areas themselves should set the alarm bells ringing. Think about it – if someone were qualified to do all the trades, they would have spent most of their adult working life in colleges or as an apprentice to gain all the necessary qualifications. So thanks, but no thanks! That is why I always recommend that you deal with each trade individually, and under a separate contract agreement.

As a starting point, here is a list of various tradesmen and the type of work they are qualified to do:

### ✏ Builder

*A builder will undertake foundation works, alterations, construction and any changes to the physical body of a property. They will also do plastering and bricklaying, although sometimes these tasks are outsourced to specialist plasterers and bricklayers.*

### ✏ Ground worker

*This chap digs the ground to prepare it for foundations to be laid.*

### ✏ Joiner or carpenter

*These guys take care of any timberwork, such as doorframes, roofing joists, floors, architraves, staircases, etc. For anything involving wood, these guys are good!*

### ✏ Painter and decorator

*The right people for the job when it comes to gloss work, exterior and interior paintwork, wallpapering, and some might also do coving.*

### ✏ Plumber

*A plumber will safely install all your pipe work; wet central heating systems, and sanitary installations (sinks, toilets, etc) in your bathroom and kitchen and lead work.*

### ✏ Electrician

*They can complete a full or part rewire, and install the necessary wiring for an extension, renovated kitchen/bathroom, etc. They are allowed to self-certify as long as they are part of the 'competent persons scheme'. They must apply for building regulations approval and must leave you with an electrical test safety certificate on completion of their works.*

### ✏ Gas engineer

*If you require a gas central heating installation or alterations to an existing system, you will need a gas engineer who is Gas Safe registered and will carry a Gas Safe card. This displays a photograph of the engineer, their registration number, and if you flip the card over, it will have a list of the types of gas work that they are qualified to carry out. You will also find a free phone number on the card so that you can contact Gas Safe directly to confirm the engineer is who they say they are. Carbon monoxide, which can be emitted from faulty or badly installed central heating systems, is poisonous. In fact, it's a killer! So make sure your engineer is Gas Safe registered. They are also allowed to self-certify so make sure they leave you with the relevant gas safety certificate.*

✎ **Carpet fitter**
*The person who puts down underlay, lays carpets and vinyl floor coverings as well as laminates and in some cases, real wood floors.*

✎ **Tile fitter**
*The person who lays floor and wall tiles.*

✎ **Window fitters**
*They can install new windows on your property. Make sure they are registered with FENSA (the Fenestration Self-Assessment Scheme) to ensure that your new windows comply with current building regulations. However, if a non-FENSA member installs your new windows they must get building regulations approval.*

# Do your research

With your list of the tradespeople you require in hand, you are ready to begin the search in earnest. But where to start? Here are a few avenues you might like to try:

✎ **Recommendations**
*Speak to friends and colleagues who have had similar work done. Do not stop with the first recommendation; try to get two or three names. One of the benefits is that you can go and have a look at work the tradesperson has completed, and as long as it is like for like it will demonstrate what they are capable of. If you are using the services of an architect or agent, they may be able to recommend a builder, but you do not need to use their recommendation. In fact, it is sometimes better to arrange your own builder so that there is no possible conflict of interest between you, the architect and the builder. They could be really good friends or even related. The problem is, should it come to dealing with problems on the build, neither can be considered impartial and it becomes two versus one with you in the minority.*

### Professional organisations

*Each trade has its own professional organisation(s), which will usually provide information on registered trades people.*

### Business directories

*As old-fashioned as it might seem, many trades still advertise in the Yellow Pages and other local business directories and local newspapers.*

### TrustMark

*To protect the public from cowboy builders and help promote reputable contractors, the government, in partnership with the construction industry, has developed this scheme. TrustMark is a publicly available register of independently assessed companies that do repair, maintenance and improvement work.*

### Internet search

*Often the fastest and simplest way to generate a list of names of local traders.*

## Performing background checks

Once you have a list of potential tradesmen (ideally at least three of each type, so that you can get three quotes), it's time to put you deerstalker on and do some investigating. There is no point asking somebody for a quote until you have checked that they are legitimate. First off, fire up the computer and type the company name into a search engine. If you are not one of the internet generation, get somebody to do it for you. A simple online search may bring up any problems other people have experienced with the company or their work in the past via online forums and so on.

If you find nothing untoward online, move onto the government's Companies House website, **www.companieshouse.gov.uk**. There you will be able to find out such information as when the company was founded and how many, if any other, businesses the owner of that company is involved with and/or has been involved with in the past. If a trader has had a string of companies, and especially if they have folded each time, alarm bells should start ringing. Another thing to look out for is that rogue traders often put their company in another person's name – they do this so that their assets cannot be seized should an unhappy customer pursue legal action against them.

The Companies House WebCHeck service offers a company names and address index free of charge which enables you to search for information on over 2 million companies. The searches can be carried out on a company either by using its name or by using its unique company registration number, so ask your trader for their number. For £1 you can also request more detailed reports, such as a company's historical information, including accounts and annual returns. To me, that's a quid well spent! There is also a free 'monitor service', which allows you to keep track of the submission of information to Companies House by any company you choose. Payment can be made by credit/debit card or PayPal and all products are delivered electronically to a unique secure download area.

## Rogue Customers

It's worth bearing in mind that while you should make all these checks for your own piece of mind, any trader you ask for a quote can also do background research on your credit rating. In fact, I would always advise a company to do a credit check on their client to make sure that they are financially stable and can afford to pay for the work. Believe it or not, there are rogue customers out there who have no intention of paying up for the work. Both parties should always do their research, no excuses!

# Getting quotes

## Quotation or estimate?

Before we go any further, do you know the difference between a quote and an estimate? Be honest. Of course I'm about to enlighten you, that's why I'm writing this book! Which, by the way, if it helps just one of you to avoid falling into the 'cowboy trap' I will be well chuffed! Here we go then.

An estimate is an educated guess at what a job might cost. However, it isn't binding. The tradesperson needs to take into account any possible unforeseen developments, particularly with any ground works, footings, etc, as well as the things that can't be seen without thorough inspection. They should provide several estimates based on various circumstances, including the worst-case scenario. This will prevent you, the customer, from being surprised by the final costs.

A quotation is a fixed price offer that can't be changed once accepted by the customer. However, your legally binding contract (see Signing on the dotted line later in this chapter) will include a seven-day cooling off period by law, during which time you can cancel the deal without incurring penalties. This is also the case even if the tradesperson has had to carry out much more work than they anticipated. If the trader feels this is likely to happen, they may possibly just stick to an estimate until they can investigate further. They should specify in the quotation precisely what it covers and that variations outside of this will be subject to additional charges.

Traders should always state clearly whether it is a quotation or an estimate.

## Requesting quotes

Your next job is to invite the trades to quote. I would always suggest getting at least three quotes, so that you can compare prices and timescales.

To work out a quote the trader will need to know his or her fixed and variable costs. These include the cost per hour of manual labour and the cost of the materials you'll require. The quote is then calculated according to what the trader thinks the job will involve. They should provide the quote in writing and include a detailed breakdown. This will help to avoid any disputes about what work is included in the overall price. They will probably set an expiry date but do not feel pressurised at any stage to make a quick decision. They may suggest that the quote will no longer be valid beyond the time limit. You can understand why they would do this because material costs may increase in the interim, which would mean the trader takes the financial hit.

Here are a few handy tips to follow when requesting quotes:

• Give each builder a copy of your plans if available and make sure that each one visits the site.
• Make sure that all the quotes reflect the same work specification including site clearance, material supply, who supplies what and who does what, etc.
• Ask for details of the required payments. For all but small jobs, the builder may ask for payments at specific stages of the work. The payments should reflect the amount of work already completed.
• Ask for a detailed breakdown in the quote – this will identify areas where money could be saved If there is a chance there could be a problem with the property, pay them to check it out.

*'Never, ever tell the tradespeople what your budget is for the work, as by hook or by crook they will find a way to spend the money for you.'*

## CASE STUDY

### *Looks like a job for poker face...*

An elderly lady I met made the mistake of revealing her budget to a quoting tradesman, and ended up paying the price. Her husband, who was the director of a large company, retired with a sizeable pension fund. Sadly, shortly after retiring he passed away. His wife decided to use the money to build a bungalow on their land. When she contacted a builder for a quote she made the mistake of telling him how much she had available to spend – and he spent every last penny of it. He lived in the property while he was undertaking the work, making phone calls and using the heating and electricity, and she was left to foot the bill. Not only that, but he made an awful job of the build. It cost this dear lady tens of thousands of pounds in remedial work, even the roof had to be completely replaced. In the end, she paid thousands of pounds over the odds of what the bungalow would have actually cost to build had she not hired a cowboy builder.

It just goes to show how important it is to keep a poker face when requesting quotes from tradespeople - never reveal your hand by telling them how much money you have available for a project.

## Comparing quotes

When you have received your three or more quotes, you need to weigh up your options carefully before making a decision and taking someone on for the job. It's not just a simple case of picking the cheapest quote. As well as the quote price and timescales, you also need to consider quality of workmanship and the behaviour of the builders.

In many cases homeowners look at the prices quoted and go for the lowest figure thinking they are going to save money. That is perfectly understandable in times of austerity. However, the risks can be high and in the long term it could turn out to be a false economy. Remember, it's not as if you are buying a domestic appliance from an electrical retailer, for instance. You have researched the brand and type you want and then go off to see who can offer you the best price for the product. The item and model will be the same whichever retailer you purchase it from. When it comes to builders, however, you are buying into individuals with varying degrees of skill and experience. Therefore, in my opinion, it's far more important that you choose the best one for your job.

If one of the quotes is widely different (either higher or lower) from the other two, try to find out why. It may not reflect the standard of workmanship - a builder with little work may put in a low quote just to keep working while a busy builder who does not really need the work may put in a high quote. Remember, too, that you do not always get a better job by paying more money.

You may find that you are unhappy with all the builders you have asked to quote – you do not need to use any of them; you can start all over again by asking other builders for references and quotes. It may seem like a real pain to have to do it all over again, but believe me, it will save you tons of pain in the long run. You have to get it right first time.

You may find yourself in a dilemma if a builder sets a deadline for an answer. Sometimes builders have a slack period between finishing one job and moving onto another in a couple of months' time, so they may legitimately offer to do yours now if you give the go-ahead immediately. Or, you may prefer to suggest moving your timescales so that they can do their next job before coming back to you, but be aware that this may entail an increase to the quoted price because of expected inflation, etc.

## Dealing directly with a builders' merchant

If you want to save money you could open an account with a builders' merchant and just pay your builder for labour costs. Why not visit several and get quotes for all the materials required for the build and then weigh up the options? It's easier than you think and you can be in control of all the receipts.

Some small reputable builders offer a 'labour only' service, which requires you to 'fund' the materials as the job progresses. The builders should be able to obtain trade prices for you and will be able to give you a separate quote for the materials so that you will be able to see the total cost at the outset.

A potential drawback is that you have to fund the materials yourself as you go along (the builder normally arranges to buy them in your name); if there has been an underestimate in materials cost, you may find the cost escalating. On the other hand, you may save money if they find they have overestimated. You are also unlikely to be left with any surplus material.

Remember that once you have planning permission and building regulation approval, you have up to three years before you even have to start the project. I'm not expecting you to wait anywhere near that long but what often happens is homeowners find the right builder for the job and when they can't start right away, they move on to someone who can. Good builders can be booked up months in advance. If a trader suggests they can start straight away, ask yourself one question – why? OK, you might just have caught them between jobs. Otherwise, in my opinion you are heading for Trouble Street. Take your time, chill out and relax with a nice cuppa, get your diary out and start planning.

# Beware of Rogue Tradespeople

When you get to the stage of approaching tradespeople for quotes, it's time to put those alarm bells onto the high alert setting. The right price is not a strong enough foundation on which to make your decision – you need to make sure that anyone you could potentially be working with is who they say they are, that they have the right qualifications, experience and equipment to do the work you're hiring them for, and most of all, that they are not unscrupulous cowboys who will without hesitation take your money and leave you with a botched, incomplete, and worse, dangerous end result. And believe me, if anyone knows it, I do – there are a lot of them out there!

## Cold callers

In the previous chapter I mentioned that during the planning application process a notification of your planned development work would be placed on websites and in the local newspapers. Lots of traders scan these sources looking for potential work. In the main I don't have a problem with it; after all, we've got to put bread on the table. However, in my experience, this is where the rogue traders lurk and it won't be long before you get the dreaded cold callers haranguing you, and a flurry of junk mail dropping through your letterbox exclaiming how brilliant each company is, how cheap they are and how they are the best people for the job in your area. Some may even knock on your door suggesting they were 'just passing by', armed with their glossy brochures and dodgy tape measures. Yeah, right!

OK, let's give them all the benefit of the doubt, but before you invite them to quote for the job, and especially if you are elderly, infirm, a single parent, a young couple or simply anyone who is unsure about how to deal with this sort of thing (I'm afraid you are all categorised to various degrees as prime targets for rogue traders) then please have somebody with you. I understand it can't always be someone with building experience but you must at least have a friend or relative – someone you trust who has gone through a similar experience of having building work done and can offer their support and considered opinion.

## CASE STUDY

### Things aren't always what they seem

A cold caller with a glossy photograph of himself duped one poor chap who got conned out of his cash. The so-called builder appeared to be standing in front of a very well-known parliament building with a shovel over his shoulder. He was claiming he had helped to build it! When I saw the photograph in question and on closer inspection, I soon realised that the shovel was brand new and had never seen any action. But the biggest clue as to why I felt this photo was fake was that the dubious tradesman was obviously standing at least 3 miles in the foreground! A clever little Photoshop ploy, me thinks. The gentle, mild-mannered homeowner fell for it though, and handed over many thousands of pounds up front. He was left with a disaster of an extension and later had to deal with this thug of a builder intimidating him to extract further money from the poor homeowner with menaces.

I cannot repeat often enough how vital it is to check the credentials of tradesmen and women – never judge just by appearance alone.

# Checking credentials

Once you have a quote you are happy with, you need to check the trader's credentials, and I cannot stress enough the importance of doing this. Tedious as it might seem, it will be worth it in the long run. Make sure you look into the following:

- **How long have they been in business?**

- **What is their company registration number?**

- **Do they hold the necessary qualifications?**

- **Do they have a company base that is separate from their home address?**

- **Do they clearly show a contact address and telephone number (a landline, not just a mobile)?**

- **Do they have liability insurance?**
  *If so, ask to see documentation so that you can contact the insurers to confirm the company are covered. Make sure it's in date. It's worth doing, because these documents are easily faked and if they cause any damage to your home or neighbouring properties, or cause injury through neglect to a person or persons therein during the course of construction, you need to know that you can make a claim for any damage directly attributed to their work.*

- **Are they the main contractor, as opposed to acting as an agent or project manager, with the intention of sub-contracting the works?**
  *In my experience, some of these so-called agents cream the majority of the total price for themselves, often in return for very doing little and then pay peanuts to the people carrying out the work. They regularly employ cheap labourers from other EU countries who*

*have come to Britain seeking employment. Often these people are inexperienced in the construction industry and know little of the UK's building regulations. The pay, working and living conditions along with a lack of health and safety planning causes the whole project to fall to pieces and in most cases leaves the homeowner well out of pocket.*

### ✏ Are they the members of any trade associations?

*Do not assume that a trader using an association logo on headed paper or stuck to the side of their van actually belongs to the association – always check first. These can be faked easily, or maybe the trader did sign up for the first year to acquire the letterheads and livery but failed to pay membership beyond the first year. There are several associations that exist to maintain good standards within the building industry. They have directories of members and will send out copies on request.*

### ✏ Travelling to you

*If the builder is not local and is prepared to travel a long distance to do the work, ask yourself why? Maybe he can't get jobs in his own area because he is well known for shoddy work?*

### ✏ Trading Standards

*Call the local Trading Standards office to see whether any complaints have been made about the trader.*

### ✏ Are they VAT registered?

*Only a very small builder (one or two staff) can avoid registration. Remember, even unregistered builders still have to pay VAT on materials, tools and equipment, vehicles and their running costs. The difference in price between a VAT-registered builder and a non-registered builder is much less than you would expect. If the builder is not registered he will be passing the VAT on as a cost. VAT free is a myth.*

### ✐ Can they provide references?

*Ask each tradesperson for two or three recent references (i.e. from happy customers for whom they have carried out similar work). Follow up the references, and be careful when drawing your conclusions, as it is not unheard of for referees to be friends or family of the builders!*

### ✐ Are they working on or have they undertaken and completed a similar job nearby?

*If possible, go and view a job previously completed by the prospective trader, preferably without them present. It must be a like-for-like job – it's no good looking at a newly laid driveway if you want them to do a loft conversion. Knock on doors and ask homeowners whether they completed the work to their satisfaction, whether they stuck to the price quoted and met the agreed timescale, what their housekeeping skills were like. (I don't mean did they do the ironing and washing up for you! I mean, at the end of each day did they keep the site relatively tidy, with no trip hazards, sharps or chemicals left lying around.) If you had a great job done you would be proud to show it off and extol the virtues of the team that helped make your dream come true, wouldn't you? If you find that the homeowner is busy or out at the time you call, leave your contact details and ask them to get in touch because you are hoping to use the same tradesperson that they employed to carry out their work. It's also worth calling in at a site where the trader is currently working if possible, to check on their standard of work in practice for yourself.*

I am telling you now, as soon as any tradesperson realises you are savvy and switched on, and prepared to ask all those questions, only the genuine ones will stick around. Good quality professionals will be happy to answer all your questions and queries as they will have nothing to hide – they will be proud of their reputation and willing to prove it. You won't see the cowboys for prairie dust and tumbleweed as they turn on the heels of their boots and head off into the sunset, quicker than you can say 'head 'em off at the pass'!

## Cowboy alarm bells

I'd like to end this section with a list of things that should set the alarm bells ringing and warn you that a cowboy trader has just ridden into town:

- **Never judge a book by its cover**

  *Time and time again I have come across homeowners who have chosen a silver-tongued charmer wearing a suit and tie on over the builder in their work clothes with the crack of their backside peeping over the waistband. As much as that is unfortunate and companies should represent themselves tidily, the nature of their work means they may be in their scruffs. So what? It's how well they do their job that matters. Builders are practical people – they might not have the best conversation skills or could be a little shy, but again, so what? Everyone must be judged on how well they do their job.*

- **Watch out for distraction techniques**

  *If a contractor comes to a meeting at your home and starts saying things like 'Isn't your dog lovely?', 'Are those pictures of your children? They look lovely', 'Oh, you don't look old enough to be a grandmother', 'Haven't you got a lovely home?', anything but give you a price at this stage, it's because they want you to fall for their charm. Well, don't! You will end up handing over your hard-earned cash and your dream and they will nick it and crush it.*

- **Pictures can be misleading**

  *Some tradespeople may carry a glossy brochure with photographs of all the wonderful jobs they have done. I don't care about glossy photos. I could get a representative to take a glossy image of a gorgeous hunk of a TV presenter who can also do modelling, place my name on the top of the folder and get myself some work. You have only got to look at the front cover of this book to realise the truth is very different!*

☞ **Be cautious of people who say that council approval is not required**
*If the builder does not wish his work to be independently inspected by the local authority, he may incorrectly advise you not to apply for planning permission.*

☞ **Do not be hurried into a decision**
*A reputable builder will always be willing to take time to discuss what you want.*

☞ **Prices that are too low**
*Cowboy builders and rogue traders will often quote a low price to obtain the work and then list items of work which they consider as extras; for example, they will claim the price quoted was just for the basic shell and that things like electrics, plastering, doors, skirting boards and so on are all extra.*

☞ **Prices that are too high**
*Conversely, cowboy builders might quote you an exceptionally high price if they think you are not going to go for the lowest price but are looking for quality. Look for a reasonable price that can stand the test of close scrutiny.*

☞ **Money up front**
*If the builders require any money before they arrive on site, think very hard before handing it over - reputable builders do not ask for money up front unless you request any bespoke materials that need to be purchased.*

# Before Work Commences

When you are fully satisfied that everything is in order and the tradespeople haven't made their excuses and left, it's time to show them what you would like to have done, hand over detailed specifications and agree the finer points of your working agreement. It's important to have all of this in place before work starts, so that there aren't any costly misunderstandings further down the line.

## Draw up a detailed job specification

No home improvement project should be started without a detailed job specification, which should include a detailed description of the materials that will be used and who will be sourcing them, along with a breakdown of all the elements of the works, specifying who is responsible for each stage, and a total price for the works. If contractors are left to carry out work from an unclear or un-detailed job specification, then later on down the line you might find out that your interpretations of the project do not quite match up. You should leave no room for such misunderstandings to occur. You should already have most of the information for the detailed specification in the original estimate or quote from the trader.

Once the job specification has been agreed and signed off by both parties you should avoid making any changes unless truly necessary, as this will incur extra costs. In fact, some traders will be glad if you change your mind about something on the job spec after work starts because it gives them the opportunity to ramp up the price for any alterations. If you do have to make any changes, get a written quote for the extra costs before proceeding. If you are not happy with the price they offer you, tell your tradesperson that you will find somebody else to quote for the extra work. In most cases, if you say this they will come back to you with a more reasonable quote.

## Signing on the dotted line

Your home is probably the largest single considered purchase you will ever make/have ever made – your pride and joy. So why, when the time comes to have work done on their homes, do some homeowners decide to allow builders and various tradesmen to carry out expensive works without obtaining anything in writing and without agreeing what exactly is to be done and for what price?

In my opinion, verbal contracts are not worth the paper they aren't written on! There may be arguments over what was and wasn't agreed, parties may forget things, and so on. Verbal agreements can be misinterpreted and are open to abuse.

A written building contract protects you, because it gives you the consent of the builder to cancel the work if it's not being done to the correct specification or within the agreed timescale. With everything set down in writing, the risk of arguments is minimised and you have a checklist of things that might otherwise be missed.

A builder with a good reputation will offer a contract anyway, and if not they will be willing to sign one that you have drawn up, because it protects the builder as well as the homeowner (see building works contract template below).

Sometimes disputes can arise if the contract has been drawn up incorrectly or weighted too heavily in favour of one or other of the parties. If the parties' responsibilities and duties are set out clearly from the beginning, the potential for mistrust and animosity can be greatly reduced.

Once the contract has been finalised and agreed by both parties, each will sign and date it, preferably with a witness present, and each party will then retain a copy of the contract.

## Agreeing a payment plan

A payment plan should also be agreed upon and written into the contract. It is advisable to draw up a breakdown of payments to be paid at specific stages of the build. You should also agree a snagging retainer of 5 per cent of the total price, which is held back for, say, one month after completion of the work subject to satisfaction. This will allow you to uncover small defects in the work after the builders have left the site and give the builder an incentive to fix them quickly. This retainer shouldn't be paid until the building inspector has made their final visit and a completion certificate and any electrical test certificates and gas safety documents have been issued. If the job is being funded by a loan that will be released to you at fixed stages of the work, make sure that the builder understands this and the actual points at which funds will be released. (See the building works contract template for an example of a staged payment plan.)

Just a word or two to the wise with regards to payment and method: do not pay cash at any time, and neither should you ever pay any money up front, unless the trader is ordering a special item that has to be custom-made for the job. Even then, I would suggest you pay for anything like that directly with the manufacturer via debit or credit card. If a builder does insist on payment up front and suggests it's for materials, start worrying, because chances are they don't have accounts with any builders' merchants. Reputable builders and trades will have at least two builders' merchants accounts, under the terms of which they are able to acquire materials and not have to pay for them for at least 30 days.

Some traders may offer a discount for cash, saying that they are not VAT registered. Avoid this offer. If the main building contractor is not VAT registered, ask yourself why. The annual earnings threshold is £77,000 before you have to be registered for VAT. If they have not earned £77,000 in one year, taking into account the cost of materials for each building job they do, they are either undertaking very few jobs each year or they are odd-job traders. If you agree to pay a trader in cash believing that you are getting a discount because the money will not be declared for tax, you are also guilty of a criminal offence and the chances are if the tax man discovers the trader's working practices and begins an investigation and researchers find out that you, as the homeowner, employed their services, you too could be liable for prosecution. Note, too, that if you are paying in cash and it is strictly 'off the books' that there will be no real record or proof of the work this builder has done for you and you will be forfeiting any guarantees on the work they have undertaken.

Once you have drawn up your payment plan, stick to the schedule of payments laid out. Pay each completed stage by cheque, banker's draft, and credit or debit card where possible, and get a receipt for each payment made. That way, every transaction is recorded and traceable.

*'Nobody likes paying taxes but it's the law of the land. Don't break it!'*

## Building works contract template

For peace of mind, you can provide your own contract. There are various building works contracts to be found on the internet; just type 'building works contract' or 'homeowner contract' into a search engine and you should discover a selection to choose from. Some you have to pay a small fee for before you can download and print them off, others are free.

You can create your very own contract for both parties to sign if you wish. Below is an outline of the basic requirements. Please note that it is to be used as a guide tool only and is not a legally binding contract. You would need to contact a solicitor to finalise the details.

### Personal information
[*At the top of the page you should have your full name, address and telephone number. Just below should be the contractor's full name and address, including home and business address where applicable, and a landline telephone as well as mobile number.*

*Next should be details of the work to be carried out on your property. Remember to add the address of the property where the works are to be carried out if it is different from your home address.*]

### Agreed total price for completed works £......
[*This is the final agreed price between contractor and homeowner to complete the works agreed. (A signed and dated copy of the original quote should accompany the contract.)*]

### Standard of materials used and quality of works to be carried out
The contractor agrees that they have fully inspected the site and that their price includes everything required to complete the works.

The contractor agrees to carry out the works to completion with competent skill, due care and attention, in accordance with current building regulations, other statutory regulations and requirements. The contractor will agree to employ only qualified and competent tradespeople and any sub-contractors to help complete the works.

The materials used for the works should be new unless the homeowner has agreed to use recycled or reclaimed materials.

## Completion date, start and finish times

The contractor will agree with the client:

Start date: _____

Completion date: _____

Daily start time _____ AM

Daily finish time _____ PM

If applicable, state how many daily refreshment breaks will take place and their duration.

## Official permission and approval

The homeowner (client) will be responsible for all planning applications, including any resub-missions, building regulations and any listed building applications where applicable. No building works should commence on the property until approval for the above has been granted.

In the case of works needing to be inspected by the local council building control officer during the process of the works and on to handing over the completion certificate, the contractor, with due diligence, must ensure open dialogue with the inspector to arrange their visits to the site at the appropriate stages of the build.

The contractor must also give 48 hours' notice to the building inspector before work begins on the site.

## Health and safety (good housekeeping)

The contractor must ensure the overall health, safety and welfare of all workers, clients, clients' family and friends, adjoining neighbours, general public and pets that are on, within and surrounding the immediate site to prevent risk of injury or damage.

The contractor will ensure 'good housekeeping' operations for the site. They will ensure that at the end of each working day the site will be free from trip hazards and rubbish; tools that are deemed sharp or dangerous are locked away; any chemical-based hazards are safely secured.

The client and contractor will decide on toilet facility arrangements either via the contractor providing portable toilets to be placed on the site or the client allowing reasonable access to their own toilets. The contractor will make sure that the facility is kept clean at all times. The contractor must not use the client's sink, etc. for cleaning brushes, paint rollers, building tools and the like.

An agreement for building waste disposal must be agreed and appropriate skip supplied to the site. It must state clearly who will be paying for the skip. If the skip is to be sited on a public highway, the council must be contacted and permission sought.

## Contractor/client liability

The contractor must show the client their liability insurance documents and confirm who the insurers are. It's up to the client to confirm that it is a current and valid document. If necessary, they should contact the insurers directly to confirm validity.

The client is responsible for notifying their building and contents insurers to advise them that construction and alteration to their property is being carried out.

It is up to the client to remove any valuables, electrical goods, furniture, etc. that could be directly affected by the works. Should any damage arise due to negligence by the contractor, they will pay the cost of replacement or repair to the item in question.

The contractor will ensure the property is secure and weather tight where possible at all times during the build and certainly on leaving the site at the end of each day, ensuring all tools and materials are securely locked away.

## Making changes [*Try not to make any!*]

The contractor will not make any changes to the agreed plans without a written agreement with their client stating any extra cost and a diagram of the new specification. Once the new plan has been agreed between both parties for the alterations, the contractor may proceed. The contractor has 36 hours to inform the client of a decrease or increase in costs due to the alteration of works.

## Payment schedule

The client agrees to pay the contractor the agreed fee to carry out the works to a satisfactory completion. The contractor will supply their VAT registration details to the client, if applicable. The client will make a note of the contractor's VAT number. The payments will be determined and agreed by either a direct debit payment from the client's bank account into the contractor's account (all bank details to be exchanged and agreed) or by banker's draft, or cheque. These will be paid in full on satisfactory completion of the works within 14 days of receiving the invoice or at a pre-agreed stage of the works as listed in the guide below. The contractor will supply an invoice to the client for 95 per cent of the agreed amount due along with itomisation of all works completed. The invoice must clearly show the VAT amount if applicable.

Staged payment schedule example guide:

Stage 1) £_____ (inc. VAT) on completion of _____
Stage 2) £_____ (inc. VAT) on completion of _____
Stage 3) £_____ (inc. VAT) on completion of _____
Stage 4) £_____ (inc. VAT) on completion of_____

Each staged payment should be paid within 14 days of receipt of the contractor's invoice unless otherwise stated within the contract.

The client should retain 5 per cent of the overall final agreed price for what is commonly regarded as snagging. Any problems arising within 30 days of the works being completed should be written down and handed to the contractor to rectify the problems if any. The contractor will be allowed 90 days from issue of client notice to rectify the snagging problems. Once these have been addressed to the client's satisfaction, the client will pay the final 5 per cent balance within 14 days of the works being rectified.

## Official documents and certificates

On completion of the works, the contractor will hand over to the client all official documents, certificates, instruction manuals, etc. relating to the completed works. For example, building completion certificate, gas and electric test certificates, etc.

## Breach of contract

Should the contractor fail to carry out the work to a satisfactory standard or fail to bring the works to a satisfactory conclusion within the agreed time frame, the client is within their rights to notify the contractor in writing that unless the problems are addressed to the client's satisfaction within the seven days of issue of said notice, the client will inform the contractor of 'intention to terminate' the contract. If the two parties fail to resolve the issues set out in the notice, the client should then write to the contractor stating the full termination of the original contract and the reasons for their actions.

The client can then arrange to employ other contractors to complete the works. The client should pay the contractor a fair price for the satisfactory works completed to date in accordance with the agreed pricing structure of the contract and taking into account the cost to the client of completing the works.

Should the client fail in their duty of agreement to make the scheduled payments on time or fail to allow the contractor proper access to the property to enable them to carry out the works as agreed, the contractor may notify the client in writing that if the breaches of agreed contract are not addressed within seven days of issue of the notice, the contractor may then notify the client of 'intention to terminate' the agreed contract. The contractor is entitled to a fair price for the satisfactory works completed to date in accordance with the agreed pricing structure of the contract and taking into account the cost to the client of completing the works.

The agreement details laid out above are a binding agreement between client and contractor.

If the above contract agreement is signed on the client's own property, the contractor must state in writing a 'seven-day cooling-off period' from date of signature, by law.

The client and contractor will both hold a copy of the above contract for future reference.

Signed _____
The Client

Signed_____
The Contractor                           Date_____

## Setting up a working agreement

When you have signed up all the relevant trades you should arrange for a group meeting to take place at the property. This will enable you to introduce everyone to each other, so that they can swap contact details and coordinate times and dates for each trade to be on site. That way nobody will be holding anyone else up and slowing the job down. Even with the best-laid plans in the world, projects rarely run smoothly. You are bound to get a hiccup or two along the way but you should at least try to prepare for every eventuality. A schedule of works chart, including a start and end date, should be drawn up and placed on a wall for all to see, including you, the homeowner.

You should also request that any tradespeople working on your property sign a condition schedule before work starts. This is a document with supporting photographs that shows the condition of your property before work begins, and should include in particular access routes that tradespeople will use to get to the working areas. The purpose of this agreement is to protect you, the homeowner, and the builder, should any damage be done during the works and an insurance claim need to be made. The work being done should only improve the room being renovated/the area being extended, and should not affect neighbouring rooms or properties. However, bear in mind that you can't include dust in this – you have to accept that any building work in your house will create a certain amount of dust. The builder should put in place dustsheets to avoid excessive ingress of dust into neighbouring rooms, but it cannot be stopped completely, and you should pack away anything valuable that could be permanently damaged by the dust.

During your meeting with the traders, the following should be considered and agreed upon, so that everyone knows where they stand:

- Which rooms of your home the traders are allowed to access and which rooms are out of bounds.
- Security on site – it shouldn't be necessary to hand over keys as I strongly recommend that you have a representative on site at all times when builders are at work on your house. However, security of stored traders' equipment might be an issue that needs to be discussed.
- Where the tradespeople can store their materials and equipment.
- Parking arrangements for the traders' vehicles.
- The use of electricity – whether traders will use a generator, or if they are plugging in to your mains supply, you should agree which power points they are allowed to use.
- Which bathroom facilities can be used by the traders (if any). Most reputable building companies will bring their own portaloo, which is by far the preferable option!
- The time work will commence and finish on each day.
- Your daily routine, as well as the builder's – you will need to coordinate on a daily basis, so that you are kept informed of the different stages taking place and how they may impact on your home life.
- The plan for disposing of the general building waste – who is responsible for hiring a skip and organising an official permit should it require to be set down on a public highway.
- Which areas should be sheeted up to minimise the dust particles coming into the living area.
- Health and safety – any building company should as a matter of course have a health and safety plan in place, which should be displayed on a wall. It should include telephone numbers of the local council, building inspector and emergency numbers, along with a list of personal protective equipment (PPE), and hazardous materials such as asbestos that they might come across during the work.

Remember, if in doubt, ask. This should ensure some peace of mind and, hopefully, a good relationship with your tradesmen.

# *Clive's Golden Rules*

- Ask friends to recommend builders, but still check them out yourself.
- Get at least three quotes.
- Pick the right expert or tradesperson for each part of the job.
- Remember that a good builder is worth waiting for – if they're not available immediately, be patient.
- Check the tradesmen's credentials, insurance and references thoroughly.
- Draw up a detailed job specification.
- Always have a written contract in place before work commences.
- Agree on a schedule of payment, and never pay for work up front.

OK, sermon over! Let's get back to the job in hand. Build on!

# Chapter Four

---

# Making Sure Your Project is a Success

So now everything is in place and the building work can finally begin. However, it's not just a case of simply handing over the keys, packing off on a two-week holiday and returning to find a sparkling new kitchen/extension/conservatory attached to your house. You've already done the groundwork by setting up clear parameters for your working agreement and signing a contract with your team of tradespeople. In order to ensure that your home improvement project is a success, you do need to keep an eye on how things are progressing and be on hand should any problems arise.

## Keeping Things Running Smoothly

If you have followed all my advice so far, you will have performed background checks, verified references and will therefore be confident that the traders you have hired for the job are trustworthy professionals. However, this doesn't mean that you should allow them free rein to access your property while the work is being carried out...

### Supervising the work

I have always found that the Great British public are incredibly trusting in this regard. In most cases, homeowners have never met the trader until they come to give a quote. You will normally only meet the owner of the company when they call round to quote – you won't have met all the labourers that they will bring along on site. I suppose it's a sad indictment of modern society to have a 'trust nobody' attitude. However, the truth is, as the old saying goes, 'trust has to be earned'.

Let me suggest a different scenario. Let's just say that a stranger knocks on your door and says, 'Can I have your keys whilst you're at work? I promise I'll look after the place.' I don't think I could print on these pages exactly what you might say! I can remember my own parents being reluctant to give me a key to the house I actually lived in when I was eighteen. So why do it with tradespeople you hardly know?

It's not pleasant living in a house whilst alterations are going on, amongst the dust and noise, and due to work commitments many people can't be at home in the day to keep an eye on things. Some people decide to take a long vacation and hope that on their return the job is complete and they can move back into a refurbished dream. In my experience, that means it's usually time to wake up and smell the debris! Rarely have I met a homeowner whose renovation job went without a hitch whilst they were away.

If you can't be at home when the work is being carried out, do you have a retired friend or relative available or maybe someone who is between jobs who you trust and who could keep an eye on the progress of the work? That way, you don't need to give the tradespeople a key. Even if you had to pay that person a few quid per day, it will save you in the long run. I realise that not everyone can afford a professional project manager to oversee the work, but if you can it's really worth considering, especially for a major project such as a house extension.

I'm not suggesting that somebody hovers over the workers constantly but just that they keep an eye on them from a distance and contact you if they think something is not quite right. It's important to keep tabs on whether the workers are sticking to their agreed working hours, following adequate health and safety and security procedures and producing quality work.

# CASE STUDY

### *Handing over the keys to the castle*

A really trusting couple that I met decided they would hand the keys to their castle over to a builder and take themselves off to a far away exotic destination for a whole month whilst their shiny new kitchen extension was being built. Just for good measure they paid £18,000 up front at their builder's request as a good will payment to ensure the job would be complete for when they got back.

The couple thought they were in safe hands and tried to relax. However, they soon realised it's not possible to relax when you fear things might go wrong thousands of miles away and you can do nothing about it. After just two days on holiday they decided to ring the builder. He of course allayed their fears, as any good rogue would. He told them that things were progressing just fine, the footings for the new kitchen extension had been excavated and they were hard-core in-filling in readiness to pour the concrete. Big smiles, a sigh of relief, quick drinky-poos on the beach and relax...

That was until they got a phone call from their neighbour the next day to ask, 'When were your builders supposed to start work?' Hello! This is the bit where I say, 'Can you hear alarm bells?!' Another phone call to the builder, and guess what? He claims the neighbour is fibbing and winding them up. Now, try this one on for size: they then ring back their neighbour of eight years and have a right go at them for telling fibs about the builder (who, just in case you forgot, is almost a total stranger by comparison). Enjoying the holiday then? Not a chance!

To cut a very long story a little shorter, they called every single day after that but in the final two weeks the builder stopped taking their calls altogether. They returned home to no builder, a back garden that was a rubbish dump as no skip had been ordered, a huge trench that was full of water outside their back door, water was leaking into the old kitchen because for some reason they had removed part of the flat roof, and the excavation work had undermined the next door neighbour's wall and it had started to crack and subside. The flooring in the house was damaged where the labourers had taken wheelbarrows and materials through the front door, into the living room and out the back door. The stair carpet was ruined because they didn't take their muddy boots off when they went up to use the loo and their lovely toilet looked like a Portaloo at the end of a three-day music festival! To top it all, their phone bill was massive because the builder was using it for personal calls, the gas bill had doubled because it was winter and the builders, bless 'em, needed to keep warm!

The builder was never seen again, the locks had to be changed and my team and I were left to pick up the pieces and give this couple the kitchen they had always dreamed of.

 *'From day one of the build, take pictures or a video of the progress. Not constantly! Just last thing in the evening when the workforce has finished would be fine. It's good to keep a visual record, just in case.'*

## Good working relations

When the build has started, you will need to work with the builder. Record the progress of the project, and keep a note of all instructions you give them and any payments you make. You should feel free to ask the builders what they are doing – any two people may interpret a work specification in different ways, so make sure that they are doing what you want. Remember, the customer is king (or queen, of course!). Be aware that any extension or other major refurbishment work on your home can cause tension and stress and it can have a knock-on effect on your home and family life, and even with the most meticulous preparation work and planning, you have to accept that things don't always progress to plan.

Here are some other things to bear in mind:

- Do not just ask the builders to do small additional items of work as you could find them on the final bill. If you need to change your work specification, make sure that it is agreed in writing along with any cost/ time implication.
- If you have a problem with a particular worker – their behaviour, quality

of work or attitude – tread carefully! If you cannot suppress your feelings, identify who the team leader or project manager is and have a quiet word with them.

- If you agreed stage payments, make those payments on time and according to the contract. (providing that the work has been done to your satisfaction, of course).
- If a dispute arises, talk to the builder and try to reach a compromise.
- If you have problems with your loan provider, keep the builder informed.
- Maintain an 'overall' view of the job, do not focus on one or two elements. If the builder is 'ahead' on certain aspects of the build, this can compensate for an area that is running behind schedule.
- Good dialogue is very important – you should keep each other updated on how things are going.
- No matter how well planned a job may be, you can't prevent the unforeseen (illness, weather, etc.) so make allowances for any such factors the builder may encounter during the build process.
- If they do a good job don't tip them – give them praise, recommend them to friends or make them a lemon drizzle cake! It's their job to produce good work that they are proud of.

## A nice cup of tea and a sit down

Wherever possible it makes sense to get on with your builder and other tradesmen. It will help keep the job running on schedule and you will get quality work and good service. However, I would caution you against being over familiar. Something I have come across far too frequently for my liking on my TV show is homeowners making tea and coffee for the builders. A trader will usually have set times for breaks and will bring their own lunch, flask, etc. They are well sorted. I have met some really soft but well-meaning homeowners on my show who made cakes and buns for the guys every single day, made them meals, or even went out and bought food for them. Here is a rule of thumb if you wish to make them a cuppa: one in the morning and one in the afternoon is fine, but don't stand around chatting! The occasional biscuit is fine, too. There you go, a simple compromise with a nice smile.

*'Be firm but polite with builders – if they know they're dealing with a strong person they will back off and not try to take advantage of you.'*

## CASE STUDY

### More tea, builder?

One particular lady made the whole workforce tea, coffee or soft drinks every single hour, on the hour! I said to her, how long did they stop for each hour? She said ooh, about 15 minutes or so. So I worked out that if they did an eight-hour shift, two hours were lost every single day! On top of that, they had an hour lunch break plus 15 minutes break in the morning and afternoon. So that was a total loss of three and a half hours each working day. What made matters worse was that they were on day rate! A job that should have taken two weeks to complete took almost five, and the job turned out to be a disaster. The builder took all her money and when it ran out, so did he, taking everyone with him, leaving the work unfinished and unsafe. Do you think they gave a damn about how well they had been looked after by this lovely lady every single day? I thought not!

## Inspection procedure

When the work begins, you, as the homeowner, or the builder must notify the local building control officer so that he or she can begin making site visits.

The inspection process works like this: the building control officer will make a number of visits to the site during the build. From a home-owner's point of view it would be great to have the inspector there on site throughout (although I'm not too sure how the builder would feel about that). Sadly, that is just not possible. However, the inspections will be scheduled at crucial stages so that they and you can be assured the work being carried out on your property complies with the current building regulations. The officer will tailor the inspections to suit the individual project and will liaise with your builder at all times.

I really can't push this next point any harder. If you have any concerns at all about your build, no matter how small that worry may be, if you don't feel the answer your builder or tradespeople have given fully satisfies you, contact the building inspector straight away and they will organise a specific inspection or arrange a private meeting with you.

# What to Do If It Goes Wrong

However well you plan a project, in many cases there can be unexpected hitches which are beyond both your and the builder's control. This might include:

• Unpredicted ground conditions when laying foundations
• The discovery of structural problems not revealed in a property survey
• The discovery of a dangerous material e.g. asbestos in a roof or floor void
• A gas leak
• A leaky water pipe
• Rotten joists

Should this sort of problem rear its ugly head, the very first thing you should do is stop the work. Speak to your builder and get them to give you a price to fix the problem – they might see it as an opportunity to ramp up the price, so tell them you will also get quotes from other people. (A word of caution on this note: many builders and trades may not want to continue the work of others without first ensuring the entire job has been completed to a high standard. This is, of course, understandable if they are to put their good name and reputation to the finished works.) Ask them how much material, man-hours and so on will be required. When they come back to you, get them to put it in writing with a signature. Do not let the builder attempt to tackle the problem or resume work until you have a signed quote that you are happy with.

*'Some rogue tradespeople will create a problem in order to charge you for the pleasure of fixing it. Be wise to this scam!'*

## Raising an issue

If you spot what you consider to be bad working practices taking place, the builders have breached your working agreement or you're not happy with something that has been done, do not ignore it! Speak to the person responsible for the work, ask questions and give them the opportunity to put the matter right. If you have followed my advice so far you will be working with professional people who take pride in their work, and with whom you have established a good working relationship, so if you approach them with a valid problem they will more than likely want to work with you on sorting it out. Given the above, in most cases you will be able to resolve things amicably – but do be sure to record any query and responses in writing anyway, and to add any agreed solution and a deadline and quoted price for it onto your overall job specification.

If you are not happy with the builder or tradesperson's response to your initial approach about a problem, don't bury your head in the sand and hope it will get better. In my experience, by doing that, your bottom is stuck up in the air and you will get financially and emotionally spanked! If a job starts off poorly, believe me the middle will be bad and the end result will be a disaster. You need to nip it in the bud and address any issues you may have. You should take the following steps:

✏ **If you fail to get the right response, don't at this stage fire them from the job or overreact to the situation**
*Remember that you have signed a contract and you do not want to be the one who breaches it. Stop all works until the issue or issues have been resolved with a restructured plan of action if necessary. Only restart the build once you are satisfied – then you can keep calm and build on.*

☞ **Make a detailed list of the work you are unhappy with and take photographs and video footage where possible**
*Also make a floor plan showing the areas of each of the defects and where the photographs and video footage were taken, and take note of the date and time too.*

☞ **Get independent advice**
*Remember, you can call upon the services of the local building control officer and ask him or her to call in to view the problem area. Most building surveyors will also be able to estimate the cost of remedial works. Seeking professional advice at an early stage will cost money but it can be worth it so that you have a clear idea of what is wrong and how much it will cost to put right. The building surveyor can also monitor remedial works and check that they have been done to a good standard.*

☞ **Make an appointment with your local Trading Standards to seek their advice on the matter**
*Go armed with all relevant documents and supporting paperwork from an independent source if you have any. Take a copy of the original contract, too. The building contract protects you, because it gives you the written consent of the builder to cancel the work if it's not being done to the correct specification or within the agreed timescale.*

☞ **Put your complaint in writing to the trader**
*Stating the problem you have with their work, showing any evidence and explaining what you require them to do to put things right (but make sure you are reasonable and fair). Write 'complaint' at the top of the letter and keep the wording clear and polite. Give them a deadline (e.g. seven days from the date of the letter) by which they must respond with a solution and guarantees. Send the letter by special delivery so that they have to sign for it and therefore cannot argue that they never received it. Trading Standards or the Citizens Advice Bureau can help you to draft a formal letter of complaint.*

✐ **Keep copies of any correspondence**
*Along with a diary of events and a record of any phone calls. Take photographs if relevant.*

✐ **Give a final warning**
*If the trader refuses to comply with your requests or does not reply to your first letter, it's time to write them a second and final letter, stating that unless they deal with your complaint to your satisfaction, and promptly, you will be forced to take further action.*

✐ **The last resort**
*If the trader once again fails to respond and they become in breach of the contract between you, Trading Standards can advise you and provide information regarding taking a legal route. This is the last resort when all options open to you have been exhausted.*

## CASE STUDY

### Make like an ostrich

A lady who had become wheelchair bound needed a ground-floor extension on the family home to create a self-contained annexe, with a living area and en-suite bedroom. Easy wheelchair access was crucial to the design plan: extra-wide doors, ramps, a disabled shower and toilet facility, electrical sockets and light switches placed at an easy-to-reach height and a panic alarm system. Plans were drawn up and duly passed by the local building control department.

The contractor hired by the homeowner on this occasion was not the cheapest; in fact, he gave the most expensive quote of the lot. She chose him because of his smart dress code, his silver tongue ('I can do everything, just leave it to me') and, most important of all, he told the homeowner he had a disabled relative and he was on the local council 'preferred list' for disabled refurbishments. This was later proved to be a huge porky pie!

Things started to go wrong right from the word go. He promised a contract that never materialised, and he requested half of the £28,000 quoted for the job up front, which the homeowner gave without question or receipt. He said work would begin within three weeks of receipt of the payment and the job would take eight weeks to complete. He started the work nine weeks late, stating he had been on holiday and that on his return he was ill. At this point alarm bells should have been ringing loud and clear – the agreed time frame had been flouted and the builder had £14,000 of the client's hard-earned cash and she had zero to show for it at this point.

The so-called builder eventually turned up one Wednesday afternoon with a labourer and began taking up the driveway to the side of the property with a pickaxe and shovel. No skip had been hired so they threw the rubble onto the front lawn. The homeowner's young daughter asked them why they were putting it on the grass and they replied it was temporary until the skip arrived. Once again, the homeowner did nothing – she didn't want to rock the boat because she had too much money invested in the project already. Her inner ostrich had taken over her thinking.

After a couple of hours' work, the contractor downed tools for the day, and when he returned five days later it was not to do any work but to ask for more money for materials. 'What about the money I've given you already, I thought you said that was for materials?' asked the lady. 'Oh no,' he replied, 'that was just a goodwill deposit to secure my services.' At this point I would just like to scream, 'WHAT SERVICES ARE THEY, THEN?!' (Sorry for shouting but I just needed to get that off my chest.) The poor lady felt that if she gave him the extra £5,000 he requested, it would get things moving, but of course it didn't. At this juncture she should have asked the contractor for her money back or at least halted the build until a contract was in place. But she was now on-board the cowboy trader's roller coaster and that ride usually ends with a request for a sick bag!

And the result of her choosing to ignore all the warning signs and burying her head in the sand? Well, the extension, if you could call it that, did eventually appear at the side of her home, with a host of problems obvious even to the untrained eye: the footings were too shallow (her postman spotted that one), the bricks used nowhere near matched the existing brickwork, the new floor was over a foot higher than the existing level of the house, a concrete ramp had been added directly off the laminate flooring in the hallway to access the new build, and the doorframe wasn't wide enough to get a wheelchair through. The builder by this time had taken all the money for the job and had left the site.

All too late a call was made to the local council building inspector to make a visit. The homeowner was devastated to hear that nobody had informed them that the build was going ahead and they had subsequently never been called to inspect the build at the various stages. An independent surveyor's report was called for and the extension was condemned. Crucially, the reports found the foundations were undersized, the extension was not tied to the existing property, and there were no cavity wall ties. There was no insulation or damp course, dangerous electrics, the existing boiler flu was not resited so that exhaust gases were flowing into the now enclosed space, the roof structure was unsafe and no plumbing or drainage was ever installed. I did feel so sorry for her because she said she had nobody to talk to and felt isolated. More important to her, she considered herself very stupid and was embarrassed to tell anyone.

The worst mistake this lady made was to keep her head firmly planted in the sand as each new problem arose – trust me, if you do this, things will only continue to get worse.

## Taking further action

If you feel you've been ripped off by a rogue tradesperson and you would like to take further action, there are a number of routes you can follow.

### Adjudication procedure

Within certain contracts there is an adjudication procedure for resolving claims and disputes that is much easier and far more cost-effective than going via the court route. It's a reasonably fast procedure, too. The dispute between the parties is referred to an adjudicator who is totally independent. They are usually appointed from within the building profession. The adjudicator acts like a judge and they reach a decision usually within 21 days. It may be necessary, however, to go to court to get a decision enforced. Again, this tends to be a quick and relatively simple procedure. There is a fee payable for appointing an adjudicator in addition to the adjudicator's own fees, which are charged at an hourly rate. Adjudication is not always the end of the matter as either party may reopen the dispute via the courts. However, this is a rare occurrence and unless you are certain that you have good cause to reopen the process once more, you could just be throwing good money after bad.

## Consulting an ombudsman

An ombudsman is an official who is appointed to investigate individuals' complaints against a company or organisation. They act as an independent judge and investigate both sides of the story in order to reach a fair solution. In most cases, for you to be able to use this service the trader in question must be a member of an ombudsman scheme. Following their investigation, an ombudsman can suggest that the trader do certain things, including: offer you, the customer, an explanation of why they treated you in the manner they did, apologise, change their working practices so that the problem never arises again with future customers, and pay you compensation.

## Trade association or professional body complaints procedure

In many cases you will find that the mere mention of getting their relevant trade association or professional body involved will be enough to put the wind up traders and prompt them to deal with your complaint. If not, then most of these organisations do have their own comprehensive complaints procedures that you can follow. A good place to search for information about trade associations is the website **www.taforum.org**

If the tradesperson you are dealing with does not belong to a trade association or professional body, you can seek advice from your local Citizens Advice Bureau (CAB), the Trading Standards Institute office, Consumer Direct or a solicitor. Remember, the latter may charge for advice in some cases.

The Trading Standards Institute runs a scheme called Buy With Confidence, which lists accredited traders. If a trader fails to resolve a customer's complaint, Trading Standards can remove them from the list – most traders are keen to avoid this, so the threat of being removed from the list might prompt them into resolving your complaint.

## Legal action

Taking a trader to court should be your last resort when all other attempts to resolve the complaint have failed. Bear in mind that if you do decide to take action via the court system, you will have to pay the relevant court fees, unless legal expenses insurance is covered on your household insurance policy. (check the small print on your policy or contact your insurers for clarification). Most traders will have their own insurance, and may also have the backing of their relevant trade association, which means that their legal expenses may be covered. You are not guaranteed a positive outcome either – there is the chance that you may never see your money again and you will end up footing the bill for the court costs on top of what you have already paid out to the rogue trader.

Most traders will respond positively to a letter that threatens court action, so do give them chance to respond before you initiate proceedings. However, there are those hardened rogues who just don't care and will have no intention of ever returning to complete the work or refunding the money you have paid.

Before deciding whether to take legal action you also need to ask yourself whether you stand a good chance of winning, whether, if you do win, there will be a good chance of you recovering the money from the trader (i.e. do they have enough assets that could be seized?), and whether the amount you are claiming for is worth the cost and time the court case will take.

If the amount you wish to recover is less than £5,000, you will be able to proceed through the 'small claims track', which is a fairly straightforward and relatively quick procedure and your chances of winning are quite high, as it is likely the trader won't turn up and the judge will award in your favour. The court will assess whether a trader has enough assets that could be seized to fulfil repayment of the amount for which you are claiming. The court will then pursue the trader for the funds, who must reply within fifteen days. If he does not, then a bailiff will be sent to recover the amount owed to you, plus the cost of the bailiff's visit.

Below are listed the court fees, which were updated on 1 March 2011. The court fee must be paid when the claim form (summons) is submitted to the court and will be added to your claim. In addition, there is now a fee to pay when a hearing is appointed. These are listed separately below:

| Sum claimed | Issue fee | Hearing fee |
| --- | --- | --- |
| Up to £300.00 | £30.00 | £40.00 |
| £300.01–£500.00 | £45.00 | £50.00 |
| £500.01–£1,000.00 | £65.00 | £65.00 |
| £1,000.01–£1,500.00 | £75.00 | £65.00 |
| £1,500.01–£3,000.00 | £85.00 | £65.00 |
| £3,000.01–£5,000.00 | £108.00 | £85.00 |

You can consult **www.moneyclaim.gov.uk** for information on making a small claim online.

If your claim is for more than £5,000, but less than £25,000, you can follow the Fast Track procedure, or if it is more than £25,000, you will have to use Multi-Track. Before pursuing this route you need to assess whether the trader will have the assets to pay up if you win. You can make an initial investigation yourself via the Companies House website, **www.companieshouse.gov.uk**, or The Insolvency Service **www.bis.gov.uk/insolvency**. I recommend visiting your local Trading Standards office and asking their advice. It is also possible to get an appointment with a judge to find out their assessment of the situation. For a claim of over £50,000, your case would be heard in the High Court.

The HM Courts & Tribunals Service (**www.justice.gov.uk/about/ hmcts**) is a good source of information worth consulting if you are considering pursuing a larger clam.

# Completion and Sign-off

Assuming that everything has gone to plan with your renovation project, or that any problems encountered along the way have been successfully resolved through dialogue with your hired tradespeople, the happy day will come when the work is completed. But before you sign off on the project and pay any final amount owed, you need to ensure that the work has been completed to your satisfaction:

• Look around carefully at all the work carried out. If there are any aspects with which you are not happy, go back to the builders or tradespeople with a list of things they will need to address before you make the final payment. When they have addressed these issues, check again carefully.
• Review the condition schedule that you all signed at the beginning of the project, and make sure there has been no damage caused to surrounding areas during the process of the works.
• Check that there is no rubbish left around and outside your home, and if the skip hasn't already been collected, find out when it will be and confirm that with the skip hire company.

## Final inspection

If you feel happy with all of the above, it's time to call the building inspector to make the final inspection. If the inspector deems the work to have been completed to a satisfactory standard to comply with the current building regulations and they are happy with the finished project, you will need to request a 'completion certificate'. This is a legal document that is very important to you and anyone who may eventually purchase your home in the future, so keep it safe. You may also need it for remortgaging, revaluation or insurance purposes.

### Self-certification

There are certain professional trades and bodies that are allowed to 'self-certificate' as part of the Competent Person Schemes (CPS). For example, Gas Safe registered engineers will issue you with a gas safety certificate on completion of works. For all electrical work, rewires, etc, the government has created Part P of the building regulations to cover the safety of fixed electrical installation work on domestic premises. It is the first time in England and Wales that the standard of electrical installation work has come under statutory scrutiny. When electrical work is carried out, the qualified electrician should complete a test of the installation and provide you with a test certificate. For more information

## Gas safety

Make no mistake – gas is a potential killer! Many people believe it won't happen to them. However, if you are one of the millions of people who reside in a property that has gas connected to it in some form or another, you are living with an ever-present danger.

If you can smell gas in your home, these are the steps you should take:

- Got to fresh air immediately
- Where possible, open all doors and windows to allow ventilation of the area
- If you think the gas leak is coming from an appliance, ensure it's switched off and do not use it again until it has been checked by a Gas Safe registered engineer
- Turn off the gas supply at the mains
- Call the National Gas Emergency number on 0800 111 999 (this can usually be found on a sticker on the gas meter)
- If you are feeling unwell, nauseous, dizzy, your head is aching, etc. visit your GP or hospital straight away for a check-up and tell them that carbon monoxide poisoning may have caused your symptoms.

It's always better to be safe than sorry, so draw up an emergency plan and display it in a prominent place in your home, maybe near a telephone. It should feature the steps included above and the National Gas Emergency telephone number, along with telephone numbers of the local hospital and GP surgery, and three local Gas Safe registered engineers. You could also save these numbers in your mobile for ease of access. You never know, that information could one day save someone's life.

on the schemes and to find out which trades are covered, visit **www. competentperson.co.uk**

Any test-certificates will have to be submitted before the full completion certificate can be issued by the building inspector.

## Signing off

So that's it. The workers have downed tools and packed their equipment away, you've checked that you are happy the work has been completed to the standard you require and you are now the proud owner of a shiny new completion certificate. Feels good, doesn't it? All that remains is to pay your traders the final snagging amount, sign off on the work and enjoy your newly improved home.

## *Clive's Golden Rules*

• If you can't be on site yourself to supervise the work, ask a friend, neighbour or family member to do so.
• Keep a visual record of how work is progressing by regularly taking photos or videos.
• Dialogue is key to maintaining good working relations with your trades.
• Never change or add to the job specification without getting a written quote for the additional work.
• By all means offer the workmen the occasional cup of tea, but don't go overboard as it could eat into the project's deadline.

- If you spot something that has gone wrong, stop work immediately and do not allow it to restart until a solution has been agreed upon.
- Get a written quote for any remedial work that needs to be done due to problems occurring during the build.
- If you aren't able to resolve a problem through dialogue with your builder, seek independent advice.
- Always try to resolve problems amicably first - legal action should only ever be taken as a last resort.
- Only pay your builder the final snagging amount once you are happy that the work has been completed to your satisfaction and you have received your certificate of completion.

# Chapter Five

---

# The Nuts and Bolts of Home Improvements

Every renovation project and home build presents its own particular issues and challenges. In this chapter I have gathered together practical tips and advice that I have gleaned over the years whilst being involved with the renovation of homes and property.

If you are installing a new kitchen, for example, you can flick straight to that section and find relevant information for your project. Even though you will be working with skilled tradesmen who are hopefully experts in the field for which you have hired them, having a good understanding of what the job practically involves will stand you in good stead and give you more confidence in your dealings with them. The information given here should, of course, go hand in hand with all the other advice I have given in the previous four chapters to ensure your project is a success.

## Loft Conversions

Unless you live underground or in a flat or apartment, you probably have a loft space that, if it's like mine, is full of boxes for old toasters, irons, kettles, TVs, old records and tapes, Christmas decorations, photographs and cards from past loves, clothes you only dream of being able to fit into again if you ever manage to stick to the diet or are keeping in the hope that one day 32-inch bell-bottom jeans with three-button high waists will come back into fashion, and so on.

If it was converted professionally, however, into a living space, it could add thousands of pounds onto the value of your home. A loft conversion can be a tricky and time-consuming job but if carried out correctly by a competent and experienced contractor, the results can be amazing. Remember, this is a very specialised area of building work so you will need to see previous examples of the builders' like-for-like work before you make any final decisions on the build team you hire for the job.

Not all loft spaces can be converted so before you get started on the planning consider the following:

• Is there enough space for the required height? Let's face it, in terms of height you are going to want to stand up in it and bear in mind that the new floor could be as much as 150–200 mm higher than your existing joists (though that would have to be confirmed on the official survey).
• Does it have potential as a comfortable and viable living space?
• Is the roof sound? Make sure you can see the felt under the tiles and that it is in good order throughout.

If all these boxes can be ticked, there is a strong possibility it could be suitable for conversion.

**The roof**
The roof structure is designed to keep all weathers at bay and to contain light loads of storage. Once it has been converted it will be able to withstand far greater loads because of alterations to the structure and flooring put in place.

Commonly there are two types of roof: trussed rafter and traditional. Trussed roofs have been around since the late 1960s/early 1970s. These are not so good if you want to convert a loft and should never be altered without first getting the opinion of a structural engineer to do all the calculations. However, it's not impossible, just a little more difficult. For example, a series of supporting beams would have to be installed to provide extra strength for the floor and to reinforce the rafters. This enables the bracing sections of the trusses to be cut out to create a more open floor plan.

Traditional style roofs are generally made up of items called purlins and rafters, which span across each load-bearing wall. These are nowhere near as complex as the trussed design. The structure will still need to be strengthened with extra joists, though, to support the new floor and extra load-bearing capacity. Once again a structural engineer's report will be required along with the design plan.

Please DO NOT try to take this job on yourself by simply boarding over the existing timbers, believing you can then start using the loft as a living space; it was never designed for anything other than light storage so if you don't want to end up down in the living room without taking the stairs and causing untold damage, leave it to the experts.

## Stairs

Talking of stairs, you will need to access your new living space with a staircase. This will be paramount to the success of the loft conversion. If you have the available space leading off the original stairwell this could save space and could be more cost effective. If not, you may well have to section off space in an existing bedroom with a studded wall partition to house the staircase.

There are certain figures and parameters to bear in mind with the inclusion of a new staircase. The maximum pitch must not exceed 42 degrees, the riser of each tread on a domestic staircase should not exceed 220 mm, and the going (the flat bit) should be a minimum of 220 mm. You will also require a clear headroom space of at least 2 m, although for some conversions the regulations will allow a reduction to 1.9 m to the centre of the stairs and 1.8 m to the edges. Handrails and balustrades will be required. The handrail should be a minimum of 900 mm in height and any exposed edges of staircase or landing will require a balustrade with a minimum height of 900 mm. Where stair spindles are required my rule of thumb is to keep the maximum distance apart to 95 mm at the widest point.

If you only have enough space to convert the loft into a single room then you can have a space-saving alternate step staircase installed. I must point out that these are steeper than a standard staircase and I believe they can be difficult to master and should only be used by healthy adults and teens. Young children or the elderly must be supervised and aided.

## Windows

Any newly created room must have windows and ventilation; this is achieved in the case of a loft conversion by way of a roof window or opening light. Remember only to use an experienced competent person to fit this type of window; if it's not installed correctly, it can cause untold damage to the property. The general rule of thumb is that the window should be around 1/20th the size of the overall floor area of the room. The window will also require highly efficient and modern double-glazed units with low emissivity glass. This technology deflects heat back into the room in winter and in summer will reflect or absorb infra red heat from outside, thus keeping the room cooler. It's also worth bearing in mind that almost 25 per cent of heat loss is through windows so do not cut corners; it could end up costing you more in heating bills.

## Heating

If you are planning to heat the new area by extending your central heating wet system, be sure that the existing boiler and pumps can cope with the extra capacity. Get a qualified plumber in to do the math in advance and remember that a qualified Gas Safe engineer must undertake any work that is carried out on a gas boiler. If you are planning on extending an electric storage heater system, once again, make sure a qualified electrician does the math on the existing ring circuit in case of potential overload. The electrician must be Part P registered or approval will be required.

## Fire safety

If you are converting the loft of a bungalow, you must ensure there is adequate fire protection and escape routes. You will need mains-powered interlinked smoke alarms on the ground floor and newly created first floor levels and you must ensure that an escape window is installed in each habitable room. The escape windows must be big enough to allow people to escape in case of an emergency and be fitted with quick release escape hinges that allow the window to open wide. Standard hinges are no good. Refer to your local building control officer or FENSA for more details.

The same applies with a similar two-storey property when it comes to fire regulations – you must fit wired, interlinked audible warning smoke alarms and escape windows. I realise it's more work but it gives you a chance of escape or rescue if the seat of the fire is affecting your means of escape via the stairs. Your expert who you will have hired to undertake the work should know all about the fire regulations, including such things as audible alarms, escape windows and fire doors will all form part of the protected escape route. It's always a good idea to fully familiarise yourself with all the regulations. It gets really tricky when it comes to loft conversions in a three- or four-storey property and the regulations, particularly on the fire safety aspect, are more complex, so once again have a chat with your local planning and building regulations departments before work commences. Also, ensure the person carrying out the work is aware of current regulations.

# Cellar and Basement Conversions

The first thing I will say here is that this type of conversion is really tricky and it can be quite pricey. Having said that, it's all relative, and done well it can increase the value of your property significantly. However, get it wrong and it can leave you in a financial black hole, quite literally! I have witnessed awful cellar conversions in my time and I've witnessed the damage to property resulting from such poor workmanship. I've also witnessed the stress and heartache the results have caused to homeowners.

So, where to begin? First off, it's your home so you must have been down the cellar once or twice? Maybe you have been using it for storage or as a workshop? Go back down again with a notepad and pen and check for the following:

- Is there decent access via solid stairs or is their space to install a staircase?
- Is it a large enough area to accommodate a decent living space?
- Can you walk around without banging your bonce?
  - You don't want to be excavating the ground level because this could have potential to undermine yours or a neighbouring property's foundations. You could also end up breaching the water table and that could lead to a high risk of flooding. Jacking up the floor above to create the space could also cost a small fortune.
- Most cellars suffer from damp, but does yours ever flood?
- Is there a window for natural light and ventilation or space for one to be created? Usually you will at least have a clay or brick style vent built into the solid wall.

Once again, if you can tick all the boxes, then you have a good chance of being able to have a successful cellar conversion.

Next, get professional advice, as this will bring to light any of the technical issues that may arise. Your local building control office in most cases will be happy to give advice through one of their surveyors.

## Damp-proofing

Due to the fact that a cellar is predominantly built into the ground it will invariably suffer with damp problems and the potential for water ingress. The remedy for this is commonly known as 'tanking'. This is a highly skilled job for the experts. In most cases the expert will use a system of waterproof render which forms a damp proof layer over the floor and up the walls. You will need a written guarantee from the company you have employed to carry out the work against any moisture ingress in the future affecting the conversion. Your local building control officer will need to visit to make sure the system being used is adequate before the work is carried out and then may request a final inspection of the completed damp-proofing works. This is also useful for your own peace of mind as the homeowner.

## Drainage

If you are thinking of having a sink, bath or shower room down there or maybe using it as a utility area, then drainage needs to be planned from the outset. Any appliances sited in the cellar conversion will need to be connected to the foul drain. However, the connection will have to be made at upper-ground floor level where the waste is usually sited. If this is the case, you will need to incorporate a macerated pump system with smaller, more flexible diameter flow pipes which makes the connections far easier, but you must plan the pipe route in advance for ease of drain connection.

## Ceiling

As far as ceilings in basements and cellars go, they are usually a case of exposed brick piers, blocks, joists and boards, unless remedial work has been carried out previously. Well, one thing is for sure, you are going to need to install a proper ceiling in order to convert it into a liveable space, and while you have the chance I would recommend that you insulate the void with sound-deadening material to a depth of 100 mm and finish off with plasterboard which has good level of fire resistance.

With regard to further precautions and fire regulations see **Fire safety** in **Loft conversion** above, but do always consult an expert.

## Heating

As for heating the new area, please refer to the information in **Loft conversion** above, but here's an extra tip for you. A good idea to save on the heating bills and prevent heat loss through the walls is to dry line the interior walls with a system of timber battens fastened to the brickwork and foil-lined, insulated plasterboards screwed on top. You'll be amazed at what a difference this can make to the overall containment of warmth. A plaster skim will be required to finish.

## Stairs

If you need to install a staircase for access to the cellar, then consider the positioning carefully. For the staircase regulations, see the information in **Loft conversion**.

# Garage Conversions

Many people have a garage that's probably never housed a car since it was constructed. It's usually full of junk – old paint tins, wardrobes, ladders and a box full of bits of old rope and string marked 'will come in handy one day'. It really is a wasted space in many cases. So, if you are in need of more living area and you can't afford to have anything purpose built, then how about moving into the garage? It's most certainly a more affordable option.

However, this can only really apply to an attached garage. Don't attempt to convert an old shabby garage, such as the ones with prefabricated concrete wall sections and corrugated roof panels. The best candidates for conversion are those constructed from brick or block with a pitch or flat roof.

## Roof

If the roof is a pitched one with a flat inner-boarded ceiling, it will require a minimum of 300-mm deep quilted insulation in a two-layer system, one layer between the ceiling joists and one laid at right angles over the joists. The roof needs to be ventilated at the eaves, too. In many cases, where flat roofs are concerned, they may well need replacing or updating to provide adequate thermal insulation.

## Walls

Some older garages built in the 1970s only have single leaf block or brick walls, in which case you would need to consider creating an inner leaf (wall) of block that is tied to the existing wall. If the new inner skin is going to be supported off the slab, use extra lightweight blocks. Or you could consider a stud wall. Either way, you need to create a cavity for insulation to save energy and help prevent heat loss.

Where the garage is semi-detached, soundproof insulation should be provided to the party wall.

If only part of the garage is being converted, both thermal insulation and 30-minute fire separation must be provided to any new dividing walls separating the garage from the room you have converted.

As part of the garage conversion, it is likely that the original garage door will need to be in filled with a new wall, which should be constructed to achieve a good insulation value. Typically, to get the maximum out of the room in terms of heat retention, a wall construction would be built out of brickwork on the outer leaf, if the main body of the garage was constructed from house bricks, and an inner leaf of 100-mm block work with a 100-mm insulation cavity. If, as I say, the main garage is constructed of single brick or block work, use those calculations for the remaining inner perimeter.

You may need to add a new window or door to the in-filled wall. You will require 2 x 100 x 150 mm concrete lintels, or 2 x 100 x 110 mm pre-stressed lintels may be used to span the opening of a single garage door. The ends of the lintels should be cut into the existing brickwork to ensure a minimum end bearing of 150 mm (check manufacturers' guidelines).

Depending on whether the foundation has been cast as deep-fill or shallow-fill (see below), there could be a small or large amount of wall construction needed below ground level (substructure), on which the above ground walls (superstructure) will be built. The principal require-ment of the substructure is to ensure adequate support is provided to the superstructure. To remain effective the bricks or blocks and mortar should be resistant to frost and also to sulphates within the ground. Undertaking such works will require building regulations approval.

**Foundations**

Foundations are required to transmit the load bear of a building safely to the ground. Therefore, all buildings should have adequate foundations; these are normally made of concrete, which will vary from one project to another depending on the circumstances of each case. These foundations can be cast as deep-fill (filling most of the trench) or shallow-fill (where the minimum thickness to transfer the load to the soil is provided). There are other types of foundation that may be used if the ground conditions do not make trench-fill practical.

As the foundation of the existing garage is not likely to be traditional (it's probably a shallow slab), a new foundation may be needed for any new walls you put in. It is advisable to contact a structural engineer or speak to building control for further advice.

Here are some factors to be taken into account of when designing foundations:

✏ **Soil**
*The type of soil that the foundation will sit on is important for two reasons: it should be able to bear the weight (load) of the foundation and the build. Different soils have different load-bearing capabilities. The way soil reacts to variations in moisture content (such as in prolonged rainy or dry seasons) can lead to it expanding or contracting. This is a particular issue with some clay soils. These changes mainly occur up to a certain depth (typically about 0.75 m), therefore foundations should be made deeper so ground movement does not affect them.*

✏ **Adjacent structures**
*It is important to ensure that the excavation for the new foundation does not undermine adjacent structures. In general, it is good practice to excavate at least to the same depth as the bottom of the foundation to the adjacent building. If the excavation runs alongside an existing footing then care will be needed - for example, by excavating and concreting the foundation in shorter sections to avoid undermining a whole length of a party wall structure.*

✏ **Trees**
*Trees can cause problems if they are close to the garage. They will draw moisture from the ground around them and beyond through their root system. As moisture is drawn from the ground it will have a tendency to shrink. How much of the ground will shrink will depend on the type of soil (clay soils shrink more than other types of soil) and the size and type of tree (both of these affect how much moisture the tree draws from the ground). The presence of trees in clay soil areas can mean foundations need to be significantly deeper*

*than might be first expected, although if the trees are far enough away, there may be no impact. If existing trees are removed or significantly reduced in size, all or some of the moisture in the root system will be released over time into the soil and, if the soil is clay, for example, this could cause expansion of the soil and damage to nearby foundations and structures supported on it.*

### ▭ Drains

*As the weight (load) from the foundation of a building is transferred to the soil it spreads downwards outside the footprint of the foundation at a typical angle of 45 degrees. If the 45 degrees within the area covers a drain or sewer there is a risk that the load from the foundation could affect it and possibly cause it to crack. Therefore, the foundation excavation should normally be at least to the same depth as the bottom of the deepest part of the drain, sewer or its trench.*

### ▭ Weight load

*The foundation will need to support more weight load from a two-storey building compared to a single storey. This is a significant factor in determining design, particularly in respect of its depth and width. This is directly related to the load-bearing capacity of the soil supporting it. The width of the foundation is also governed by the wall thickness. Some properties have been constructed on landfill sites, which may require a more extensive form of foundation, such as underpinning, as the depth of undisturbed ground could be many metres deep. An alternative may be a 'raft' foundation.*

## The floor

The existing garage floor is likely to be strong enough for general domestic use, but may need to be upgraded to ensure it is adequate in terms of damp-proofing and thermal insulation. It may also be desirable to change the level of the floor to match the levels in your existing home. The simplest way to achieve this would be to upgrade the existing concrete floor. Alternatively, if levels permit, a new timber floor could be constructed over the existing concrete floor.

The concrete floor can be used as a base; however, a new damp proof membrane (DPM) will need to be introduced. Damp proof membranes come in solid or liquid form, the latter being a better solution for a garage conversion. A suitable gauge damp proof membrane (DPM) and thermal insulation must be provided. These can be laid over the sand blinding or on top of the concrete. Thermal insulation may be required and can be placed on top of the membrane (if a liquid membrane is used, care should be taken to ensure the two materials do not react with each other – a separation layer may be needed). The exact details will vary depending on which products are used, so check with the manufacturer and always get an expert's opinion.

The floor can be finished with a layer of screed or a timber covering known as a floating floor, the exact specification of which will depend on the insulation material used beneath. A screed is likely to need to be around 75 mm thick and should include a reinforcement mesh to prevent it from cracking. Care should be taken to ensure any existing airbricks for the main house are not obstructed by this work. If so, they should be extended through the new floor to external air.

The existing floor level of the house may be quite high above ground, and in cases such as this it is more effective to use timber joists to raise the floor, with a void underneath. A minimum gap of 150 mm should be kept between the existing concrete floor and the underside of the timber. The timber floor joists must be sized correctly depending on their length. They should then be laid across the shortest span from wall to wall with a gap underneath.

An intermediate wall with a small footing may be needed to reduce the span and keep the thickness of the floor joists to a minimum. A damp proof course (DPC) should be placed on the underside of the timber. Insulation is then placed between the joists. Air vents should be placed in the external walls to provide ventilation to the void and the air should be able to travel from one side of the building to the other.

## Windows and ventilation

If the access to the converted room is from another inner room linked to the existing property then a specially sized window must be fitted with an unobstructed opening of 750 mm high by 450 mm wide. The sill height should be no higher than 1,100 mm from floor level.

Each new room in a house should have adequate ventilation for general health reasons. The type of room will determine how much ventilation is required. When inserting a new internal wall you need to be careful not to make the existing ventilation worse. If a new room is being created as a result of the addition of an internal wall then care should also be taken to ensure that the existing room is ventilated adequately. There are two main methods of ventilating a room:

**Purge** - this is achieved by opening the window. The opening should have a typical area of at least 1/20th of the floor area of the room served, unless it is a bathroom, which can have an opening of any size.

**Whole building** - this is also known as trickle ventilation, which can be incorporated in the head of the window framework, or by some other means. The area varies depending on the type of room. A bathroom, for example is 4,000 mm. All other rooms are 800 mm.

Both of these forms of ventilation are normally required; however, alternative approaches to ventilation may also be acceptable, subject to agreement with building regulations. Consult your local building control office for further information.

# Party Walls (civil law)

In England and Wales, if you wish to carry out work on your property that may affect your neighbour's property, you must make sure you comply with the Party Wall Act 1996. If you intend to make any changes to shared walls (whether they be internal or external), floors, ceilings, driveways or other shared spaces, you may need to gain written approval - and sometimes even planning permission.

The Party Wall Act allows you to carry out some work on adjoining walls in flats, and terraced or semi-detached properties without permission. For example, you can put up shelving, plaster and rewire, etc, as long as it does not exceed above half the width of the wall, ceiling or floor. It is advisable to warn your neighbours if the work is likely to be noisy, or they may make a formal complaint to your local authority under the noise laws.

Below is a simple guide for you to follow if you intend to carry out works on a party wall:

• Write to the neighbour or owner of the property you share the wall with to give notice before any construction work begins (try to give two months' notice). You will require proof of delivery, so send it recorded, or if you deliver it by hand take an independent witness with you and make a note of the date and time of delivery. I know this sounds very formal and you may have known the neighbours for years but it's best to keep things official just in case.

• If you live in a flat or apartment, you will need to check your lease for what work you can carry out. Then write to the freeholder for advice/permission to carry out the work you want to do. Ensure you get a written response within fourteen days; don't rely on a verbal agreement.

• Do not begin the work if the owner/neighbours haven't bothered to respond, because you could be in breach of the act and this could result in everything being placed into dispute. If there is a dispute, a surveyor can be appointed jointly or separately and he or she will award in favour or against the work you want to carry out. Should it result in a no verdict, you have fourteen days to appeal to a county court. Should it ever get to this point, it may be worth reconsidering whether it's worth the hassle and the right type of home improvement to make in the first place. Even if you are lucky enough to get a yes, some unhappy neighbours can make jobs that affect their property very difficult to carry out, so try to get it all agreed in writing first.

# Re-roofing

After a period of time your roof may need replacing, or maybe you purchased a property and were advised to replace the existing roof. In most situations, this work will need building regulations approval.

The replacement or alteration of the roof could affect how the roof works and cause movement to occur. Movement could cause cracks to appear in the walls and, possibly, the eventual collapse of the roof. When performing work on any roof, care should be taken to ensure the roof will continue to perform effectively and without any movement.

If your existing roof needs replacing, it's very important to make sure that you employ an experienced, competent person to carry out the work. Replacing a roof can be a costly and pretty messy job to have done and it's vitally important to get the job done right first time. Remember that roofing work can affect your neighbours, particularly in terraced and semi-detached properties where the party roofs are joined together. Scaffolding has to be rigged up in most cases and a full health and safety assessment and checks must be carried out.

If the new roof is to be replaced with a different material to its original (for example, slate to cement-based roof tiles), then approval under the building regulations is likely to be required to ensure the roof will be adequate in terms of structural stability, in particular where the replacement tile will be significantly heavier or lighter than the existing one. It will also have to meet fire safety and energy efficiency requirements of the building regulations.

As a roof is defined as a thermal element, the new one should have improved thermal insulation values to prevent against heat loss. Insulation can be placed between the ceiling joists. Again, the thickness will vary depending on the material you choose to use. If the roof has no ceiling then the insulation can be placed between the rafters and ventilation must be put in place; therefore, the ridge should also have vent tiles installed to allow for flow-through ventilation.

Here is a list of structural elements and identifying tags for a typical pitched roof:

- **Ridge boards** form the apex of the roof and where the rafters are fixed to both sides.
- The **rafters** are timbers that create the main pitch of the roof and support the tiles and battens.
- **Purlins** are long pieces of timber that are usually seen halfway along the rafters and act like beams to reduce the span of the rafters.
- **Struts** support the purlins and are fixed at an angle with one end connected to the purlin itself and the other on to a load-bearing wall or a timber spread across ceiling joists. These are the diagonal timbers seen in the roof.
- **Ties** help prevent the roof from spreading and form the familiar A-frame shape. They can either be the ceiling joists or can be fixed halfway up, usually above the purlin, and are fixed horizontally from front to back (common in terraced houses).
- **Ceiling joists** can act as ties, but mainly support the ceiling below. They are usually relatively small in size and they will not be able to take the load of any typical room used in a house. The rafter timbers that make up a pitch roof will naturally attempt to spread apart (called 'spreading'). Ceiling joists prevent this action from taking place. They are attached to the base end of the rafters and stop them from pulling apart.
- **Wind load** – The roof needs be tied down to the structure to stop it from lifting when strong winds prevail. Attaching straps that are just over 1 m long with a cranked end usually achieves this. The strap is attached to the wall plate on which the roof timbers are secured to the inner leaf of the wall at 2-m fixing centre intervals.

### Ventilation and insulation

It's a common misconception these days that all roofs require ventilation. It is not the case if you are installing a 'warm roof system', which is where the insulation is placed above the joists or rafters. However, ventilation will be required for a 'cold roof system'. When ventilating a roof the air should be allowed to flow freely by entering into the void at one end and exiting at the other.

In regards to a 'warm deck' installation, the insulation is positioned over the rafters and then felt is placed on top. The battens and tiling are then secured down over it. The thickness of the insulation will vary depending on the manufacturer's specification.

With a 'cold deck', the insulation is usually positioned in-between the rafters or it can be placed between the ceiling joists. Once again, the thickness of insulation in either case will vary depending on the material used and the manufacturer's specification. The roof should have vents installed along the eaves to both front and rear or from side to side. In the case where the insulation is placed between the rafters, vents should also be placed along the ridge.

# Installing a New Kitchen

When it comes to planning a kitchen, size really does matter. In most cases you can only work within the space you have available. My first rule of thumb is to know exactly the floor area. I have a saying that I call the four 'Ms' rule. It goes like this: measure, measure, measure and just for good measure, measure again! It's critical that you get that bit right to begin with. You need to account for floor area, ceiling height and any permanent fixtures like boilers, cookers and where the doors are positioned in the rooms. You don't have to be a technical drawing wizard either, just a basic pencilled sketch will do. Remember to take your tape measure with you to the suppliers or DIY outlet so that you can begin to have an idea of what will fit and what won't.

## Shape

You also need to understand what shape of area you have. They all have their pros and cons:

- The G-shape encapsulates and surrounds you and uses lots of worktop space. It usually links the kitchen to a breakfast-bar-cum-dining-area.
- The galley style is very efficient, but worktop space can be limited – certainly not a kitchen where you will find lots of people at parties.

You can strategically place a nice mirror or two to give the feeling of extra space and volume.

• The L-shape is very popular in the UK and is very easy to plan and design.

• The U-shape surrounds you with appliances and worktop space. Ideal for an island, if the space allows.

### The working triangle

When considering your layout, it is important that you plan the working triangle correctly (see diagrams). This is something that was born out of professional working kitchens. As you prepare food, you move between three areas for washing up, cooking and retrieving cold-stored food: your sink, cooker and fridge-freezer. This is referred to as the work triangle. Make this an essential part of your kitchen design. You also need a place for preparing the food. The best place for this is within the working triangle. It maybe a worktop on an island, or between the cooker and fridge-freezer.

The best thing to do is ask a representative from a kitchen company or DIY store to make a visit to your home and create a plan that best suits you and your kitchen type and shape. Many companies are able to scan your kitchen and produce a digital plan with accurate measurements that will allow you to visualise what can fit in the space. It should be a no obligation visit, so do not be pressured by hard sales talk into signing on the dotted line. You can take your printed diagram and shop around until you get exactly what you require and at the price you want to pay.

It's a good idea to point out on the diagram exactly where you would like electrical sockets to be positioned. In the case of any gas or electrical work to be carried out, you must use qualified professionals to undertake such work and make sure you get safety certificates when the work is complete.

Remember that any new kitchen with no opening window or window light should be provided with a mechanical extractor fan to reduce condensation and remove smells.

*'Kitchen companies tend to change their display suites to reflect the new season's trends and ranges on a regular basis - if you find out when this is due to happen, you can go in and ask to buy an old shop display suite for a knockdown price. Don't be afraid to haggle! Please ensure, however, that with a little jiggle here and there, it will fit your space.'*

# Installing a New Bathroom

When planning your bathroom or en suite, many of the same principles that I mentioned in the kitchen section apply. Consider the following:

• Is the bath going to be a stand-alone or, if you are tight for space, do you require a shower over it?
• What type of wash-hand basin and toilet would you like?
• Would you like to install a bidet?
• Are you happy with the location of each unit or would you like to move things around?
• If you just want to update the suite without moving any items that is fairly straightforward. However, bear in mind that if you are changing the positions you will require the plumbing and pipe work to be replaced or extensions to be made to the existing system.

Take your measurements carefully and put them down on paper, then sketch where you would like each item to be placed. Remember to make a note of where the windows and doors are positioned before you head off to your local bathroom specialist or DIY outlet. An extractor fan will need to be installed if you haven't already got one to help get rid of the excess humidity, steam and help prevent condensation moisture build-up. If you have a window close to the bath, make sure the unit has toughened safety glass just in case you slip or fall and put your hand out to stop yourself. If you are having a new electric shower fitted, please make sure a qualified electrician installs it. They will also check that all the copper pipes are correctly earthed. If you are having light fittings fitted directly above the bath or shower, remember to ask your electrician if they need to be Zone 1 fittings.

There are a couple of issues to consider when installing downlights in a bathroom. Firstly, the ceiling is part of your home's fire protection, so when you make a hole in it for the downlights it's important to consider whether 'fire-rated' downlights are needed – if there's accommodation above, for example. Also, if there is insulation in the void it'll be necessary for the downlight to be protected from this, otherwise it could overheat and cause a fire. I think it's always a good idea to protect them with a fire hood which can usually be purchased with the fittings.

Bathrooms are classed as a 'special location' because of the high risk of shock where humans, water and electricity may collide. Two additional things to consider – the requirement for an RCD (residual current device) protecting the circuit(s) into the bathroom, and IP-rated light fittings to protect against moisture. If you have seen the initials IP on a light fitting and never understood what they mean, you are about to be enlightened! It means ingress protection. The numbers associated with the IP letters relate to the level of moisture protection the light fitting has. Remember, water and electricity do not make good bedfellows. I'm only giving you this information so that you can ask your qualified electrician some questions and get them thinking, how the heck do these homeowners know so much? If you ask them nicely, they will explain what all the zones mean, 0, 1 and 2, etc. I recommend it if you suffer from insomnia; you'll be fast asleep in seconds!

Just one final point on bathrooms. If you intend to tile the walls or floors, make sure you buy a really good quality tile adhesive and grout which are waterproof and flexible.

## CASE STUDY

### *If the bath fits...*

When it comes to planning a bathroom be realistic about size – don't start getting delusions of grandeur and ordering a huge bath and shower tray before you've checked your floor space measurements accurately.

One lady whose home I visited had ordered a bathroom suite online via a well-known auction site. The problem was that the items were way too big for the space she had available. Unperturbed by this she had insisted that the plumber install them anyway. He had to chop into the walls to make the oversized jacuzzi bath fit and the shower tray was snug up against the toilet and pedestal. There was a 228-mm wide gap down between the edge of the bath and shower tray, which meant that only someone the size of Twiggy could access the sink and toilet! It was like negotiating an obstacle course. The door to the bathroom wouldn't even open halfway because it hit the shower cubicle.

The lady realised the error of her ways even before it was installed but she knew that the seller on the auction site wouldn't accept returns. I was amazed I found someone who would fit the suite in the first place. The whole thing was a disaster from start to finish to be honest. The builder drilled a hole from the bathroom to the lady's bedroom to plug the jacuzzi bath into the socket on the bedroom wall. The enclosure had a leak and the water seeped through into the bedroom via the electric cable! The toilet pan was not fixed to the floor so she was rockin' all over the world whenever she sat on the loo and to top it all, she was getting an electric shock every time she went to turn the tap on.

No forward thinking or planning took place here, and of course, no reputable plumber worth their salt would ever have taken the job on anyway as soon as they realised the suite was way too big to fit the space available. I suppose there is always one who sees an opportunity and grabs it. Needless to say, it all had to be ripped out and a suite designed for the space was finally installed. In my book, that's expensive ignorance!

# Removing a Chimney breast

I'm a huge fan of older properties and especially those with real open fires. Every home I grew up in and have subsequently owned has had at least one room with a real fire. In fact, the bigger the fireplace, the better. There is a certain magic to sitting in front of a real fire, watching the flames flicker and the glowing embers generating the warmth. It has a real romantic charm about it that you don't get cuddling up to a loved one in front of the radiator! The truth is, of course, that the setting of a fire in a fireplace is a dying art and nobody enjoys having to clean out the ash pan. More importantly, these days homeowners are looking to create more space in their homes without actually having the added cost of extending or the hassle of moving altogether. Chimney breasts can dominate a room and use up a lot of floor area. Years ago houses were constructed with fireplaces in every room to provide heat. Over the years central heating has replaced the need for fireplaces and the chimney breast is seen as a waste of space in the room. Although a fireplace does provide a focal point, the removal of the fireplace and the chimney can increase the size of the room significantly.

### Retaining structural support

In most cases, the chimney is part of the structure of a house and removing one requires careful consideration. Don't just think you can take a big lump hammer to it and expect there to be no serious consequences to your actions. The upper floors, walls and sometimes the roof of a house may be supported in some way by the ground-floor internal walls. Removing these walls without inserting an RSJ (rolled steel joist) or beams, etc. to support the structure above could result in undermining the whole property and cause damage or even result in partial or total collapse of the building. If a ground-floor chimney breast is removed and suitable supports are not provided to withstand the weight of the stack and chimney breast on the floor above, the results could be catastrophic. The unsupported stack and breast could send the walls crashing down to the floor below, endangering life and limb.

The work must comply with current building regulations. Where the chimney is part of the party wall adjoining two properties, the Party Wall Act 1996 places certain responsibilities on the person intending to carry out the work. (See Party Walls section in this chapter.) The best practice is to employ a specialist in this kind of building work and remember that a structural engineer will be required to carry out accurate calculations for the correct sized beams to be installed. It is possible to remove chimney breasts from the flank or party walls of a property without actually affecting the strength of the existing wall, but you should still have a structural engineer involved from the word go, for peace of mind more than anything else. In some instances they may suggest that a buttress wall or pier be installed in place of the chimney breast.

The cavity, where the hearth and chimney breast have been removed, may require the existing floor joist hearth trimmers to be removed and replaced with full-length floor joists to take the load bear from floors and ceilings.

## Retaining the chimney stack

Should you wish to keep part of the chimney above the roof (whether that be due to a listing regulation, a planning permission stipulation or purely for aesthetics) it will need to be supported. If you decide not to remove the chimney stack, you will need to get the top capped off to prevent water ingress. Otherwise, it may need to be vented top and bottom. There are many ways of adequately supporting a partially removed chimney. However, you must make sure that whichever way you intend to carry out the work, it must comply with current building regulations. The best method would be to install an RSJ or steel beam and post system or a gallows bracket.

# Chapter Six

## Can You Do It Yourself?

**So you've got a job you want doing in the house – is it time to DIY (do it yourself) or GSI (get someone in)? With the right tools and following my handy tips, sometimes you can get the job done yourself rather than hiring people for the simple stuff.**

# The Gadget

OK, so you want to hang a picture on the wall or maybe put up that spice rack in the kitchen that's been hanging around for years. Or maybe a floating shelf floats your boat? And what about the TV bracket to mount your new flat screen on? Well, don't just grab the drill, point it at the wall and shoot – not unless you fancy an instant new shocking hairstyle or worse when you drill through a live mains cable! Or there could be a water pipe lurking beneath, just waiting to soak you and the furniture as your drill bit penetrates the pipe. All in all, this DIY job could end up costing you a fortune.

So, how do you know exactly where the live electric cables and water pipes are then? The answer is, take two twigs about 10 inches long and hold one in each hand, cross them over and stand against the wall. If they separate away from each other you know there's water present... I'M KIDDING!! Who knows, though, I've never tried it, so don't knock it!

There is a far simpler way to check these days and it comes in the form of a hand-held gadget that's been on the market for years that no toolbox should be without. It's called a 'metal and voltage detector'. You can buy them from any good DIY shed. In fact, I recently treated myself to a new one so that I could demonstrate this top tip on my TV show. Prices vary but mine cost just £14 from a well-known store and it even had a stud wall detector on it, too. This is a great addition because most new houses have stud partition walls (they have a hollow sound when you tap on them). A stud-dividing wall is made up of a timber studwork frame covered in plasterboard with a plaster skim. The problem is, it's difficult to detect correctly where the timbers are located, and if you want to hang something substantial on a stud partition wall, you'd want to drill into a solid piece of timber rather than just plasterboard. This clever little device detects the centre of each piece of timber and takes the guesswork out of it.

Different brands may vary slightly in design, but my metal and voltage detector has a simple three-position switch system, which allows you to detect mains voltage, metal pipe work and of course the timber stud. There is a green light that indicates no detection, and a red light alerts the user to the presence of voltage/pipes/timber beneath the surface, allowing you to avoid/target those areas as appropriate. There is also a different audible warning for each one.

*'A metal and voltage detector is a little beauty that costs little but could save you a fortune. In my opinion, it's a must have for any DIYer.'*

# Driller Thriller

I love this tip - it's so simple but so effective. In fact, this is a load of tips for the price of one. (I'm good to you.)

Follow this easy step-by-step guide to a DIY 'driller thriller' (I'm easily excited!) if you want to drill a hole in the wall at home to hang a big picture, or put up the wall mount bracket for your flat-screen TV, or, just to make things interesting, if you want to drill through a ceramic tile in the kitchen or bathroom.

The tools required for the job are:

- Metal and voltage detector
- Cordless or corded drill
- Tungsten carbide masonry bit (or specialist tile bit)
- Bradawl
- Depth stop or electrical tape
- Plastic wall plugs
- Screws
- Spirit level
- Rubber mallet
- Marker pen
- Masking tape
- Ooh yeah, and an old envelope (tell you about it later)

Most wall bracket fixings will come with an installation guide and usually the wall anchors and fixings. So let's say you need to install a loo roll holder in the bathroom or toilet, which has a tiled surface. Before you get started I will say that we are told from a very early age that 'practice makes perfect', so if you have never drilled a tile before it might be a good idea to practice on a damaged one first, either clamped to a board or workbench.

The first thing you need to plan is where you would like to site the bracket. (For a loo roll holder, close to the toilet is a good idea!) When you have decided on the position, get your metal and voltage detector and run it over the area to make sure no danger lurks beneath. Then, offer the bracket up to the centre of a tile, hold it against the wall with one hand whilst resting a spirit level on top to make sure your holder will be level when you have completed the job. Get someone to hold the level for you if you don't feel you can do two things at the same time. Once you are level, hold the bracket firmly in place and mark each hole clearly with a marker pen and remove the bracket.

Now for the envelope. I first used this tip a few years ago on my TV show and the amount of mail I got about it was astonishing! It doesn't have to be a new one; it can be one that had that morning's junk mail in it if you like. First, fold the flap back, then take a strip of masking tape and place it along the length of the back section of the envelope, leaving half the tape exposed to attach to the wall just below the bracket marks. When it's firmly in place, pucker out the front pocket of the envelope. If you haven't guessed yet, it's to catch the debris that will be made when you are drilling. This simple but effective tip prevents the dust debris getting caught up in grout joints, textured wall coverings, etc. When the job is done, gently remove the envelope and bin it.

The next job is to get the bradawl and, holding it firmly quite close to the tip, gently apply pressure over the pen marks you have made and make a tiny scratching motion until the glazed surface has been penetrated on each marker point (be patient). This gives the tip of the drill a location mark to prevent it slipping and sliding like Bambi on ice. Some people prefer to use a square of masking tape (which you can see through) placed over the pen mark to prevent slippage, but it's a bit hit and miss in my opinion.

Now, take the correct size tungsten carbide tipped masonry bit (preferably a new one) and lay it down on a flat surface, then take the correct nylon wall plug and lay that down alongside the drill with the tips level with each other. Take the electrical tape or depth stop and attach it or wrap it around the drill bit as a reference point for the length of the wall plug. It's always a good idea to add an extra 5 mm so that the plug sits just under the surface of the tile or plaster depth. This will indicate how deep you need to drill. Place the drill in the chuck and tighten. Make sure your drill is not in hammer mode until you have fully penetrated the tile and only then if the masonry underneath is proving a little tough as the percussion hammer action could cause the tile to become unstable or break. Place the tip of the bit onto the scratch mark and gently squeeze the trigger. Allow the drill and bit to do the work, do not apply too much pressure.

When you have successfully drilled the holes, push the wall plugs in and tap flush with a rubber mallet (it's best to use a rubber mallet because if you miss with an iron hammer it may break a tile). Pop the screw into the plug, give it a couple of twists then gently tap the head of the screw to push the plug beyond the depth of the tile - this is because if it's flush with the tile when you come to tighten the screw, it will place pressure around the diameter of the plug and could crack the tile. Put the bracket in place with screws but do not over-tighten. Remove the envelope and bin it. Hopefully, job's a good 'un!

## Get to know your drill

Drills are so inexpensive these days so every home should have one. It's worth getting to know your drill – like, 'Hello, drill, my name is  ' Don't be daft. I'm kidding again! I mean how many speeds has the motor got? Does it have hammer action (which is a must if you are drilling into solid masonry)? What size chuck does it have (10–13 mm, etc), is it keyless or do you need a key to tighten up the chuck?

Here's a quick guide to nylon wall plugs, their colours and sizes, and which drill bit size is required for each, and which screw size:

| Nylon Plug | Drill Bit Size | Screw Size |
| --- | --- | --- |
| Yellow | 5 mm | 6–8 |
| Red | 6 mm | 8–10 |
| Brown | 7 mm | 10–14 |
| Blue | 10 mm | 14–18 |

Remember, if you make the hole too big, the plug will just spin, so follow the guide for a snug, safe fit.

# Fixing a Dripping Tap

Every homeowner at one time or another will have experienced a dripping tap somewhere around the house, but what they might not realise is that left unattended it can waste thousands of litres of such a precious resource...Water. If you are on a water meter it costs you even more. Nine times out of ten, the cause of the problem is a perished neoprene washer, which is easy to fix if you feel competent at DIY. So stop being a drip and fix it!

First of all, shut off the mains water supply to the tap. If you look under the sink, bath panel or behind the pedestal of a washbasin you should find an isolating service valve on the copper pipe feeding the tap above. You will notice it has a slotted screw head that you will need to turn anticlockwise with a slotted screwdriver to shut off the water to the tap. Once you have done that, switch the tap on to make sure no water is flowing. If you do not have such a valve you will need to find the main stop tap that controls the water supply to the whole house and turn that off by hand. It's always a good idea to familiarise yourself with where it is anyway in case of emergency.

Before you begin to tackle the job make sure you put the plug in the drain hole. *Why do I need to do that, Clive?* I hear you cry. Well, because you will be taking apart the tap assembly, which has tiny parts and screws, and if you drop any of them it's very likely they are going straight down the plughole! You'll thank me for it later.

There are a few variants when it comes to taps in your home but the main ones are the traditional rising and falling spindle type and the non-rising spindle. You may also hear them called bib or pillar taps. Anyway, to you and me, they are taps! (Don't nod off yet, we're nearly at the end!)

If it's the rising spindle you will see in the centre of the tap a little plastic disc indicator (blue = cold, red = hot). On the non-riser it's a larger plastic circle with an indicator trim around the edge. Whichever it is, you gotta flip 'em out by using a small slotted screwdriver around the edge to give you leverage. This will reveal a concealed slotted retaining screw head. Remove the screw and keep it safe. It may be a good idea to line each item you take off along the top of the sink and then work in reverse order when you come to fit the tap back together.

Lift off the top section of the tap - in the case of the rising spindle you will need to remove the bell type housing to reveal the headgear nut. To undo the nut you will need an adjustable wrench. Adjust the wrench so it fits the headgear nut firmly, and place one hand on the tap spout to stop it from moving whilst undoing the nut with your other hand. If the nut won't budge, spray some water dispersant fluid on the nut and let it soak in for a few minutes, then try again. Once you have undone the nut, remove the internal tap assembly and you will notice, near to what is commonly known as the jumper valve, a small neoprene tap washer. It will probably be crushed and split where it has been tight to the seat of the tap. Sometimes you may find they are held in place by a small grub screw. If so, just remove the screw and flip off the washer with a flathead screwdriver, or you may find it just falls off anyway.

Neoprene tap washers can be purchased from any good DIY shed or plumbers' merchant. It's best to buy a mixed size pack. Replace the washer with one of the appropriate size and reassemble the tap head carefully. It's good practice to grease the threads before assembly. Once you are satisfied the job is done well, make sure the tap is in the closed position before turning the water back on. Check that the tap is not dripping and then turn on the water flow. If all is good, give yourself a tap on the back...Get it?... Tap on the back! Oh, please yourself.

# Sealing Porous Brickwork

Bricks can act like sponges and soak up moisture, particularly with older properties; this can lead to the ingress of damp into your home. Another problem is that when the damp within the bricks and the mortar lines freezes, it can cause the mortar to crumble and the brick faces to blow out; this is known in the trade as spalling. It's worth checking your brickwork on a yearly basis for any problems. If you do spot a spalled brick you need to address the problem quickly by either refacing it with a strong mortar mix or removing it completely and replacing it. If the mortar is crumbling you need to rake out the loose material and repoint the joints.

There are silicone-based products on the market that create a barrier to repel moisture, and these can be painted or sprayed on. The solution can be purchased from leading DIY outlets, builders' merchants and painting and decorating retailers or wholesalers. The good news is that once you have applied the solution it still allows the brick to breathe and therefore the moisture already in the brick will dissipate and dry out naturally.

Preparation is key to this work. Make sure you give the walls a good going over with a wire brush to get rid of any flaky and loose debris. Replace or repair any spalled bricks and repoint mortar joints that require attention. You will need to mask and cover windows, doors, frames, etc. If you do get any on the glass, wipe off with white spirits as soon as possible. It's a good idea to sheet up the surrounding floor area, too. Remember that your safety is paramount so make sure you have somebody at the foot of the ladder and it's securely tied off. If you are using scaffolding, make sure you secure yourself with a safety harness (the hire company can supply them). In both cases, do not work alone when you are operating at height.

Once the preparation has been carried out and the risk assessments completed, you can now begin the application.

Pour the silicone barrier mixture into a bucket, or paint kettle if you are going to apply with a paintbrush. Make it a good size brush, preferably about 6 inches wide. Slap plenty on. If you sense that the solution is soaking into the brickwork quickly, slap another coat on before it has time to dry. You can also use a sprayer to apply the solution but once you start it's best to keep the sprayer going and complete the job in one hit as the nozzles can clog up, so don't stop for a long tea break. If this occurs, empty out the solution and pour in some white spirit, this should clear the nozzle jets.

It can be time consuming but once it's done it will create a really good moisture barrier for your brickwork and home.

# The Mortar Mix

I've seen so many people get this wrong, including so-called professionals. I can even look at some of today's new build properties and see quite clearly that the mortar lines throughout the brickwork vary in colour and on occasion quite dramatically! I think it looks awful and when you consider the cost of a new home it's unacceptable, too. I've known some fantastic brickies who seem to get the mix right every time yet never seem to use anything other than the shovel method for measuring out the mix and I guess that has come with experience. It's a bit like when your mum bakes a cake and appears to just throw everything together and yet it always comes out brilliantly (well, at least it seemed to with my mum).

Building and construction is best left to the professionals, but if you want to put in, say, a raised bed or small wall in the garden and you feel confident enough to construct it, you are going to need to mix mortar. Here's a very simple method of getting the mix right every single time. You will need to measure out the mortar mix ingredients by simply using a builder's bucket. You will also need a spot board to mix your mortar on; this can be an old cut-off piece of ply board or you can buy a plastic version designed for the purpose from your local DIY outlet or builders' merchant.

Perhaps you will have heard builders use such terms as three and one, four and one, five and one, etc, when it comes to a mortar mix calculation. They are referring to the ratio of sand to cement. Mortar mix ratios vary depending on the type of job you are doing; ask your builders' merchant or an expert for advice.

For argument's sake, let's say you need a five and one mix. You will require five parts builder's sand and one part cement. To begin with, if the bucket does not have internal measurement marker lines, I would make a line inside the bucket at around the two-thirds full mark. Of course, it really depends on how big the task you are doing actually is. You don't want to be mixing too much for a small job or too little for a larger project. So mark the bucket accordingly. Use a shovel to fill the bucket up to the line with builder's sand. Pour the contents onto the middle of the spot board or into a mixing bath, and repeat five times. Finally, fill up to the mark with cement, and pour it out over the five parts of sand. Start to dry mix the two ingredients together using a shovel or trowel.

Once you have thoroughly mixed the two parts together, hollow out the middle of the dry mix with the tip of your shovel or trowel so that when you look down over the top it looks like a sports stadium with all four sides built up and bare spot board visible in the middle. Fill a watering can with water and begin to pour into the middle of the mix until it reaches about one third of the way up the walls. Gently begin to landslide the very top of the dry mix from all the way round into the water until it's absorbed. Mix thoroughly with your shovel until you have a uniform colour blend. The consistency should not be too wet or too dry – it should just about be hanging on to your trowel without dropping off. If the mix is too dry, add water slowly until you get the right consistency.

Many builders will use an additive called plasticiser in the mix which enables the mortar to have greater adhesion, reduces the risk of cracking and crazing, and slows the drying process without affecting the hard set whilst allowing you to play the mix for much longer. It can be purchased at your local DIY shed or builders' merchant. Just follow manufacturer's recommendations when adding to your mortar mix.

*'Don't mix too much mortar at once; in my opinion you will only get around two hours max before your mix goes off, so take it easy, you can always mix more later.'*

# Laying Floor Tiles

You will probably believe that a project like laying floor tiles should be left to the professionals. However, if you are keen on DIY and up for the challenge it can be really rewarding, as long as you are patient, have the right tools for the job and follow these instructions carefully.

Here is a list of tools and materials you will need for the project:

- Metal and voltage detector
- String and chalk
- Good quality pencil
- Straight edge
- Claw hammer
- Spirit level
- Rubber mallet
- Trimming knife
- Felt-tip pen
- Good quality, motorised tile-cutter with diamond-tipped cutting wheel (can be hired)
- Notched adhesive float
- Rubber-bladed grout paddle
- 50 mm x 25 mm timber batten
- 50-mm nails
- Bucket
- Large sponge and several clean cloths or rags
- Floor tiles (always order 10 per cent more than you need in case of breakages)
- Waterproof, flexible floor adhesive
- Waterproof floor tile grout
- Tile spacers (they come in various thicknesses, depending on what size grout gaps you would like)

It's really important to get the setting out right before you begin laying ceramic floor tiles. If you are laying the tiles on a wooden floor, you need to make sure that the existing floor is solid, with no loose boards. Be sure to check the position of hidden mains water pipes or cables below the original floorboards using the metal and voltage detector before you begin. Next, you need to lay a weatherboard marine ply base of around 9 to 12 mm. This provides a good solid surface that will prevent the tiles from cracking and the grout from crumbling between the joints due to movement of the existing floorboards. Secure the plywood sheets with screws at around one every 250–300 mm fixing centres. Remember to avoid any pipes or mains electricity cables.

You can lay ceramic tiles on top of clean concrete floors or old existing tiles as long as they are securely fixed, and make sure they are clear of grease, dirt or grime. It's also a good idea to score criss-cross lines into the original tile to allow the adhesive to get a good key hold.

Find the centre of the floor by measuring the midpoints of each wall. Get the string good and chalky, stretch it between each point nice and tight and then lift the string up in the middle as if you are stretching the bow of a bow and arrow, then release. It will leave a chalk line across the floor. Do that for the width and the length of the room and where the two lines cross each other will be the perfect centre point of the floor, giving you four even quarter sections. Place one tile in the centre point right angle between the lines and dry lay enough tiles to fill one of the quarters by working your way out towards the walls. Remember to use the tile spacers and dry lay as many full tiles as possible.

Dry laying the tiles first allows you to judge how many you are going to need for each section and to see how wide the edge gap will be around the perimeter. Cutting narrow strips off ceramic tiles is difficult, so you want to avoid very narrow edge pieces, or ones that are almost a tile wide if you can. If the edge gaps look like they are going to prove difficult, the answer is to shift the whole tile layout by the width of half a tile. Cross out the original guidelines and draw new ones, parallel to them but half a tile's width away. Lay out the tile rows again in order to check they fit. Keep adjusting until you are totally happy with the layout.

If you are laying tiles that are offset with varying sizes, here's a top tip for you. Try to dry lay the whole area first. Once you have created the pattern you want to achieve with the full size tiles and placed the spacers in-between, take a piece of chalk and number them individually on the face of the tile in large digits, then get a camera or video and take shots of the dry lay so that you have a definitive mapping system for where each one goes on the plan. You could even take a wide-angle photograph, print it off and keep it with you as you lay.

Now, a lot of experts suggest that you tile in each quadrant by working your way from the centre point to the outer wall. The problem I have with that is, if the room is quite large, like a kitchen area for instance, you will at some stage in the process have to reach over the newly laid tiles and maybe you might lean or kneel on one by accident and create an uneven floor. So here is my top tip. Nail down a timber batten at the wall perimeter where the cuts are going to be at right angles to the wall and butted up to the edge of the dry lay of tiles. The timber battens need to be 50 mm x 25 mm, cut to the required length and nailed lightly to the floor. If you leave the nails proud, you can pull them out easily later on but try not to get snagged on them. Health and safety, you know!

Once your perfect preparation has been done and you are confident with everything, it's time to begin. Start by laying the tiles in one of the quadrants that is farthest away from the door. Take your notched tile spreader and spread roughly a square metre of adhesive on the floor surface. Using the notched edge of the float create even ribbon-like strips of adhesive. Place enough tiles and spacers down to cover the area of adhesive. Work in straight lines from the outer wall to the right angle centre point line of that quadrant. Once you have laid, say, nine tiles, get the spirit level and gently lay it across the tiles to check that they are level and even. If not, tap gently on the offending tiles that are out of line with the rubber mallet until the correct level is achieved. Remember to put the tile spacers in place on each side of every tile to enable you to achieve grout uniformity. If you have excess adhesive pushing up through the tile gaps, try to gently remove it with a blunt knife or small scraper but try not to nudge the tile in the process. Once the quadrant is filled with tiles and you are happy they are all level, repeat the process in the remaining three areas completing the final quadrant by the door exit and leave to dry. Gently wipe off any excess adhesive that has appeared on the tile face by using a large damp sponge, which you should keep nearby in a bucket of water just in case. The door at this stage may not be on its hinges because you will have raised the floor level significantly and will need to plane the bottom of the door to allow it to open and close properly.

Allow at least twenty-four hours for the adhesive to dry, even if it is rapid set, maybe longer if you are laying the floor in cold conditions. Once dry, you can now walk on them, which will allow you to remove all the tile spacers. Keep them safe because you can reuse them for future jobs now that you are confident. Carefully remove the nails in the battens with a claw hammer and gently lift off the timber battens.

Next thing to do is measure up your perimeter for each quadrant and cut the tiles to fill the perimeter gaps with the tile cutter. A motorised wheel cutter is the best tool for cutting floor tiles successfully but you must read the manufacturer's operating guidelines and you must wear personal protective equipment at all times, like safety goggles, gloves and overalls. When all the pieces have been cut, laid and allowed to dry, remove the remaining spacers around the cut tiles and get ready to grout the whole area. Do this about one square metre at a time, remembering to push the grout deep into the gaps between the tiles with the grout paddle. Remove any excess with the damp sponge and this will usually smooth the grout lines too. Once you have covered the whole area, allow to dry and finally polish over the surface with a dry cloth; you may have to repeat this action a couple of times.

Once complete, stand back and admire your work, you DIY guru you!

# How to Make a Stud Partition Wall

What if your family has grown and you now have more people than rooms in the house? Or maybe two of the children who once shared a room have grown up into teenagers who want their own space? Or do you want to have an office but can't afford to extend your property? Never fear, Clive is here, and I have the answer: non-load-bearing stud partition walls. I have to point out at this stage that you will need decent sized rooms to begin with if you are going to partition them off, so that in the case of the bedroom, for instance, it can be equally shared. You will need less space for an office, though.

If you fancy yourself as a bit of a DIY guru, or you are just competent enough to follow the instructions, here is what you need to do. A stud partition wall is made up of a timber studwork frame covered in plaster-board with a plaster skim. All the necessary ingredients can be purchased at most good DIY stores or builders' merchants. You will need:

## Tools
- Electronic pipe and cable detector
- Tape measure
- Pencil
- Claw hammer
- Nail gun (optional)
- Plumb line
- Hand saw
- Electric mitre chop saw (optional)
- Power drill/driver
- Bevel-edged chisel
- Wooden mallet
- Spirit level
- Square
- Work bench
- Safety goggles
- Wood plane

## Materials
- 4x2 softwood timber
- Timber noggins cut to size
- 100mm skew nails
- No. 10 screws and wall plugs OR frame fixings
- Plasterboard
- Insulation

When you are buying the timber from a timber merchant or DIY store, make sure it is as straight as possible. Timber can swell and shrink with changes in temperature, and if it has been stored incorrectly it can twist and bend. Here is my easy tip for checking the timber before you buy. Select the piece you want, leave one end on the ground and hold the other end in the palm of your hand. Offer the end in your hand up to one eye so that you are looking down its length and while closing the other eye you will be able to check for any deformity in the timber. My saying is: 'Give it the wink to check for a kink, if it's straight, you're alrate!' (That's my northern speak for all right but all right didn't rhyme!)

OK, back to the project, Clive!

Let's say we are going to split a bedroom up. Bear in mind that if you are doing a direct 50/50 split, it will mean that you will only be able to gain access to bedroom two from bedroom one unless you section off a small corridor within the original space to access the second bedroom.

The first thing you need to do is find out where the electricity cables and water pipes are in the room you wish to partition off. They could be lurking in the line of fire just under the floorboards or in the ceiling void. This is where our old favourite the metal and voltage detector comes in handy. Remember that it also has a stud finder setting, which will be a great help for locating floor and ceiling joists.

Measure up and find the central point of the bedroom, locating the position of joists in the ceiling roughly where you want the partition to be. If the joists run in the opposite direction to the intended new wall you will be able to fix what is commonly known as a head plate (a piece of wood nailed or screwed to the ceiling, which then creates the top support for your partition wall) to each joist at approximately 405-mm centres using 100-mm oval nails. If the ceiling condition is not too good and likely to be damaged by the action of hammering, it may be best to use screws. Cut the ceiling plate to the required length from a piece of softwood timber measuring 75 mm x 50 mm. If the ceiling plate runs at right angles to the existing joists simply nail or screw it directly to them.

If the partition runs parallel to the ceiling joists you may need to lift the floorboards or boards in the loft above and insert additional joists or sections of wood at the anchor positions (noggins) into which you can secure the head plate. An easier option might be to move the partition slightly so it is directly under an existing joist. It will of course mean that one room will be slightly smaller than the other.

Once you have the ceiling plate timber secured in place, you will need to position the sole plate. Measure and cut the sole plate from the same type of timber used for the ceiling plate. Make sure it doesn't run across the foot of any doorways you are planning, and ensure that the sole plate timber is directly beneath the ceiling plate timber by using a plumb line. This is a weight suspended on a piece of string that will give you a precise reference line (you can use a portable laser line gadget if you prefer). When you have the sole plate perfectly in line, you need to fix it securely to the floor. If you are fixing it to a wooden floor, use 100-mm nails driven into the floor joists where possible. If you are fixing it to a solid floor, use 100-mm screws at around 600-mm fixing centres.

Starting at the end of the sole plate that is farthest away from any doorway you require in the stud wall, measure in 25 mm and mark the sole plate with a pencil. Now measure 600 mm, or 450 mm if using the narrower type of plasterboard. Continue to make marks at 600/450 mm intervals along the length of the intended partition line. Chances are your stud partition will not divide equally into 600/450 mm sections. If it does, you can count yourself lucky. When you get to roughly the area where you want a door or opening to be, make the mark and then add 25 mm and make another mark. This is where you can cut the sole plate to allow for the door later. Marking out in this way will help to reduce the number of plasterboards you will need to trim later on. Make sure you know how wide the door and lining is going to be, mark this on the sole plate by notching or marking the timber and then continue to mark out the 600-mm fixing centres for the studs on the other side of it. You can cut the sole plate out for the doorway later.

Measure the distance between the head and sole plate at the point where each stud will sit. Make a note of the length each stud needs to be next to their marks on the sole plate. You really want each stud fitting between the two plates as tightly as possible, and there could be some variations in the floor to ceiling height, particularly in an older property. Cut the stud timbers and begin to fix them in place. Begin by fixing to the wall. Keep the first timber stud as tight to the wall as you can, making sure it is as straight and upright as possible by using a spirit level. If the wall you are mounting it to is uneven, use timber off-cuts, known as packers, to fill the gaps between the stud and wall. Secure the end studs into the wall as well as into the sole and head plate timbers using the correct length nails. You can of course use screws and wall plugs. The stud timbers should be nailed into the sole and ceiling plate securely by nailing diagonally through the bottom of the stud and into the sole and ceiling plate timbers.

When it comes to securing the stud timbers on either side of the doorway, make sure you leave enough room for the lining and an extra couple of millimetres to give yourself some leeway when you eventually want to hang the door. The lining for the door, or the casing as it is sometimes known, should be the same width as the studs plus the width of the plasterboard on each side. This usually adds up to an extra 100 mm. Fit a noggin of timber above the door opening, known as the door head, and support this with a small vertical stud in the middle of the span, unless you plan to put a pane of safety glass above the door to help give extra light to the room without the main window. The noggin of timber must be high enough to accept the door casing.

When the stud timbers have been securely fixed in place, you will need to give the frame some extra strength. Fixing horizontal noggins between all of the studs can do this. These should be fixed halfway between the floor and ceiling.

The stud on either side of the frame should have the correct fixing centres to make locating them when fitting the plasterboard an easy job. They need to be placed wherever the sheets of plasterboard are to be joined together and must be in the centre of the join including above the frame of the door.

Cut noggins to fit between the studs and nail them in place roughly halfway up the frame, and where heavy items are later to be hung on the wall. Before fitting the plasterboard, it might be worth soundproofing the cavity with sound-deadening insulation material; this will also retain warmth in each room.

Fit the plasterboard, ensuring that each sheet is perfectly vertical and that adjacent sheets meet at the centre of a stud. Offer up the sheets of plasterboard to the framework so that they touch the ceiling rather than the floor. A skirting board can be used to conceal any gap at the bottom. Secure the boards with plasterboard screws at 300-mm fixing centres at positions all around the perimeter and the central studwork. Apart from when you are fixing in the corners of the plasterboard, I would suggest fixing centres of around 200 mm. The screw heads should be screwed in just below the surface so that they do not protrude.

Once all the boards are secured in place you will need to tape up the joints with plasterboard adhesive and scrim tape. This is a job that the plasterer can do in preparation for the plaster skim finish – I've not included instructions on how to apply plaster skim as I feel this a job best left to the professionals.

All that should be left to do now is putting the door trim around the reveal, hanging the door and fixing the door furniture, making sure the room has ventilation if there are no windows, fitting electrics, lights, sockets, switches, and so on, making provision for heating, and finally painting, carpeting and adding furnishings.

# Job Done!

I really hope you have found the book enlightening and helpful. I hope I have helped you cut through some of the red tape too.

If you prepare properly, do your research thoroughly, keep everything legal and above board, be patient and plan ahead, don't bury your head in the sand if things begin to go wrong and keep open dialogue with all parties involved in your project, I'm pretty certain that, whatever your property plans in the future, they will be successful ones.

Good luck and thank you so much for buying my book.

*Clive Holland*

# Useful Resources

### Architects Registration Board (ARB)

The UK's statutory regulator of architects. The website includes a searchable online public register of around 33,000 architects, all of whom have met the ARB's standards for education, training and practice.

*020 7580 5861*

*www.arb.org.uk*


### Chartered Institute of Building (CIOB)

The international voice of the building professional, representing an unequalled body of knowledge concerning the management of the total building process. CIOB members are skilled managers and professionals with a commitment to achieving and maintaining the highest possible standards.

*01344 630 700*

*www.ciob.org.uk*


### Citizens Advice Bureau (CAB)

This charitable organisation provides free, independent, confidential and impartial advice on a host of topics, including legal issues and consumer rights. Visit the website to locate your local office.

*www.citizensadvice.org.uk*


### Companies House

The UK's Registrar of Companies, an organisation that stores information about all limited companies in the UK. One of the resources on the website is the WebCHeck service, which offers a searchable Company Names and Address Index which enables you to search for information on over 2 million companies free of charge.

*0303 1234 500*

*www.companieshouse.gov.uk*

### Competent Persons Register (CPR)

An online searchable resource of all of the contractors in the building services industry who have been assessed as being competent by a government authorised certification scheme. Contractors on this register are regularly assessed to the standards of their sector and able to self-certify their work as meeting the requirements of the building regulations.
*www.competentperson.co.uk*

### Council of Mortgage Lenders

A not-for-profit organisation and the trade association for the mortgage lending industry. Go to the consumer section of their website for advice on mortgages.
*www.cml.org.uk*

### The Fenestration Self-Assessment Scheme (FENSA)

FENSA is the leading body providing building regulations compliance for homeowners replacing windows and doors. The organisation works with thousands of double-glazing contractors in England and Wales.
*020 7645 3700*
*www.fensa.co.uk*

### Guild of Master Craftsmen

A trade association. Member craftsmen are required to submit confidential references from satisfied customers, along with meeting certain other criteria. Only when the guild is satisfied that the applicant really does deserve to be called a master craftsmen is the application approved. The guild provides a free checking service for customers to validate a tradesman's claim to membership: *www.findacraftsman.com*.
*01273 478449*
*www.guildmc.com/consumer*

### HM Courts & Tribunals Service

Provides information about the UK's courts and tribunals system.
*www.justice.gov.uk/about/hmcts*

### The Insolvency Service

You can perform a free search on this website to find out whether an individual has ever been declared bankrupt/filed for insolvency.

*0845 602 9848*

*www.bis.gov.uk/insolvency*

### Local Authority Building Control (LABC)

LABC is the member organisation representing Local Authority Building Control departments in England and Wales. Its membership includes over 3,000 professional surveyors and support technicians throughout 12 regions. It promotes the design and construction of buildings that are safe, accessible and environmentally efficient to comply with the building regulations.

*020 7091 6860*

*www.labc.uk.com*

### The Money Advice Service

An unbiased source of advice on all financial matters, with section dedicated to mortgages and homes on their website.

*www.moneyadviceservice.org.uk*

### Money Claim Online (MCOL)

HM Courts & Tribunals Service online service for claimants and defendants; a convenient and secure way of making or responding to a money claim on the internet.

*www.moneyclaim.gov.uk*

### National House-Building Council (NHBC)

The leading warranty and insurance provider and standards setter for UK house-building for new and newly converted homes.

*0844 633 1000*

*www.nhbc.co.uk*

**Planning Portal**

The government's online planning and building regulations resource. You can make planning permission applications through the website and also find a wealth of information about the process.
*www.planningportal.gov.uk*

**Royal Institute of British Architects (RIBA)**

Membership of the RIBA is recognised the world over as a symbol of professional excellence. The organisation provides standards, training, support and recognition for their members.
*020 7580 5533*
*www.architecture.com*

**Royal Institution of Chartered Surveyors (RICS)**

An independent organisation with around 100,000 qualified members, the RICS sets and regulates the highest standards of competence and integrity among its members and provides impartial, authoritative advice.
*www.rics.org*

**Trade Association Forum**

The Trade Association Forum encourages the development and sharing of best practice among UK trade associations. It has an online searchable directory which provides comprehensive links to information on UK trade associations and the business sectors they represent.
*www.taforum.org*

**Trading Standards Institute (TSI)**

The professional association which represents trading standards professionals in the UK and overseas. It aims to sustain and improve consumer protection. Trading Standards is a local authority service. Online help may be available through your local trading standards service website for both consumers and business. Use the website's post code search to find your local office.
*www.tradingstandards.gov.uk*